Shadow Work EVOLUTION

Why Jung Followed the Freudian Fears!

Uncovering the Roots of Shadow Psychology Theory and the Rebirth of the Psyche.

> "One does not become enlightened by imagining figures of light, but by making the darkness conscious."
> ~ Carl Gustav Jung

By

Jason A Solomon, B.Ed

© 2025 Jason A Solomon, B.Ed
All rights reserved. No part of this publication may be reproduced, distributed, or transmitted in any form or by any means, including photocopying, recording, or other electronic or mechanical methods, without the prior written permission of the publisher, except in the case of brief quotations embodied in critical reviews and certain other non-commercial uses permitted by copyright law.

For permission requests, contact the publisher or author through official channels.

Title: *Shadow Work Evolution: Why Jung Followed the Freudian Fear!*
Author: Jason A Solomon, B.Ed
British English Dictionary
First Edition: 2025
ISBN: 978-1-7638935-8-0
Paperback cover design and interior layout by Aussie Guy's Books

This is a work of nonfiction. Any references to real people, living or dead, are intended purely for educational and illustrative purposes. The fictional character is entirely invented and does not represent any real individual.

> *"I am confident that you will often be in a position to back me up, but I shall also gladly accept correction."*
> ~ *Sigmund Freud*

So wrote Freud to Jung in 1907, during the height of their intellectual alliance. What followed was a rich but ultimately strained exchange of letters over eight years, letters that would later reveal the emotional and philosophical unravelling of their relationship.

The eventual publication of this correspondence offered the world an intimate view of one of the most pivotal, and fractured, partnerships in the history of psychology.

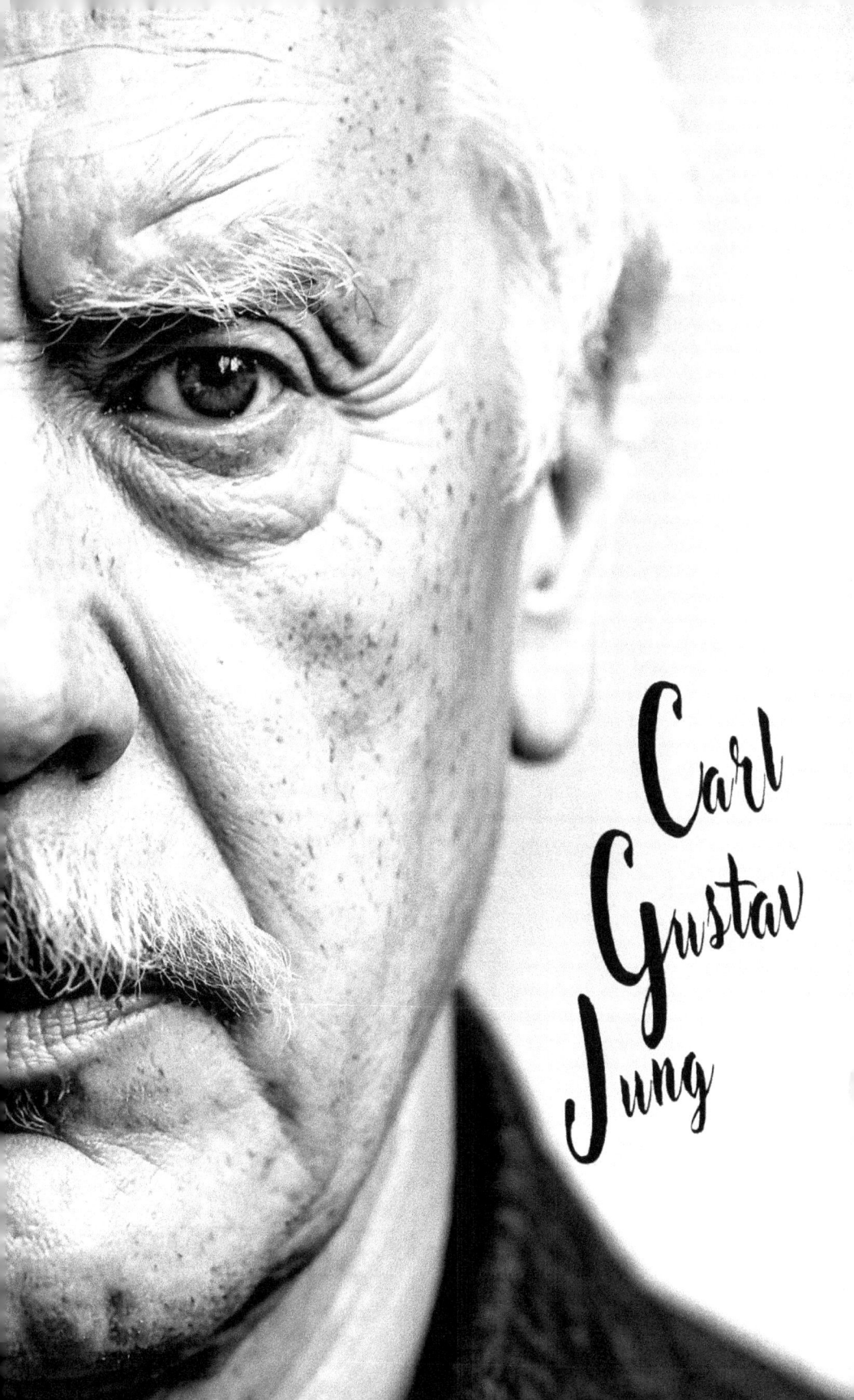

Preface

The Echo of the Forbidden Self

When I began my Bachelor of Education in the early 1990s, the study of psychology was stitched tightly into the curriculum. It was presented as essential, foundational knowledge for understanding student behaviour, human development, and the inner workings of the classroom.

And so, like many others, I met Freud first.

We explored repression, ego structures, and childhood drives. We studied the Oedipus complex with clinical detachment and were taught to see human behaviour through a framework of biological impulses, familial rivalry, and unfulfilled desire. Even then, something about it felt cold, more diagnosis than dialogue. More pathology than potential.

But what struck me most wasn't Freud's dominance., it was the silence that surrounded Jung.

Carl Gustav Jung, the man who once sat beside Freud, who challenged his teacher, who chose the soul over the symptom, was absent from the room. Not just lightly skipped. Omitted. Entirely.

It wasn't until years later, after two decades in education, mentoring both students and staff through emotional crisis, burnout, and self-discovery, that Jung's name reappeared. Not in a classroom, but in a conversation. Then again, in a journal. Then again, in a dream.

When I finally followed that thread, through the collective unconscious, archetypes, shadow work, and the notion of individuation, it felt like I was being reintroduced to something I had already known. Not learned. Known. Jung hadn't simply extended Freud's work. He had deepened it. He followed the fear. And in doing so, found the path to wholeness.

This book is the one I wish had existed on my shelf as a student. Not as a critique of Freud, but as a reconciliation of what was left unsaid. It is a bridge between repression and integration, between pathology and possibility.

You'll meet both men here, not just as theorists, but as human beings. You'll meet a fictional character, Harry, whose emotional struggles bring their ideas to life. And perhaps, in Harry, you'll meet a part of yourself.

Most importantly, this is a book about evolution, not just of shadow psychology, but of our understanding of what it means to be whole.

If Freud taught us what we repress, Jung taught us what we reclaim.

This is the journey of both.

And maybe, it's yours too.

~ Jason A. Solomon, B.Ed

Shadow Work AI Companion

As you journey through these pages, you may feel a pull to go deeper, to ask questions that are difficult to frame, or to hold a mirror to parts of yourself that resist ordinary reflection. To support you in this process, I have built the **Shadow Work Evolution AI Companion** - a compassionate, knowledgeable guide that walks beside you as you explore your inner world.

This companion draws upon the teachings of Carl Jung, Sigmund Freud, and the lived insights of my own *Shadow Work Evolution* manuscript. It has been designed to respond with empathy, clarity, and reflection, offering you a safe conversational space to explore the unspoken layers of your psyche.

> *"Your visions will become clear only when you can look into your own heart. Who looks outside, dreams; who looks inside, awakes."*
> ~ Carl Jung

My Shadow Work AI Companion is not a clinician, nor is it to be used as a diagnostician, but rather an educational and reflective partner that can help illuminate hidden corners of thought and behaviour.

The language it uses is flowing, gentle, and non-judgemental. Each exchange blends academic rigour with accessibility, offering you both the grounding of psychoanalytic theory and the warmth of a human-like presence.

Whether you want to unpack a dream, consider a recurring emotional pattern, or simply ask "why does this keep coming up for me?", the Shadow Work Evolution AI Companion can hold that space.

Think of it as a mirror and a lantern: reflecting back what you bring forward, and illuminating paths you may not yet have considered. It is yours to use whenever the pages of this book stir something in you that needs more room to breathe.

You can explore it here:
https://shadow-work.ai

Or

Scan the QR Code

Contents

Preface 7
Shadow Work AI Companion 9
Two Men with One Mission 13
Building the Mirror 15
The Psyche According to Freud 18
The Psyche According to Jung 22
The Great Divide 27
The Birth of the Shadow 30
From Myth to Method 33
Projection and Pain 36
The Rise of Integration 40
The Archetypes Within 46
Beyond the Shadow 55
The Rise of the Inner Revolution 62
Soul, Symbol, and the Sacred Psyche 74
The Collective Shadow and Cultural Healing 78
Integration in Practice 81
Echoes of Repression 93
From Shadow to Symbol 109
Post Reading Reflection 115
The Mirror of Harry 119
Endnotes & References 122
Glossary of Terms 125
Symbol Index 132
Comparative Symbol Index Table 136
Reflection Questions 138
Frequently Asked Questions 140
Afterword 147

The shadow is not a punishment. It is a portal. And naming is the first step through.

Two Men with One Mission

And the Unconscious Between Them

Long before they became opposites, Sigmund Freud and Carl Gustav Jung were mirrors.

In the early 1900s, they stood side by side at the edge of a psychological revolution. Together, they dared to ask questions others avoided:

Why do we dream what we do?
What lives beneath our thoughts?
And what happens when the parts of ourselves we try hardest to suppress begin to take the lead?

They weren't just building theory; they were building a movement.

When Freud first wrote to Jung in 1907, his tone was open, even deferential:

"I am confident that you will often be in a position to back me up, but I shall also gladly accept correction."

In the years that followed, the two would exchange hundreds of letters, filled with enthusiasm, philosophical speculation, clinical analysis, and subtle psychological tension. They were allies in exploration. Teacher and student. Colleagues. Friends.

For a time, they believed in the same mission: to chart the hidden landscape of the human mind.

Freud brought precision. He mapped the psyche into structures, the id, ego, and superego, and developed the first formal language for what we now call the unconscious. Jung brought symbolism, depth, and spiritual reach. He saw patterns beyond pathology. He saw myth in memory. And he believed that what was repressed might also be *redeemed*.

This book begins there, not at the fracture, but at the formation. Because to understand the evolution of Shadow Work, we must start with its original purpose: To meet what is hidden in ourselves and survive it.

You may be reading this because you've heard of Shadow Work as a practice. You may associate it with trauma healing, journaling, or even pop psychology. But before it became a hashtag, #ShadowWork was born from this collaboration: Freud's clinical realism and Jung's mythic vision, two lenses on one inner world.

In the pages ahead, you'll follow that world as it splits, through philosophy, through theory, and through one fictional man named Harry. His life will serve as a case study of what happens when repression runs deep… and what becomes possible when we are finally willing to turn inward.

- This is not a textbook. It's a psychological map.
- One side leads to survival.
- The other, to integration.

Shadow Work didn't begin as a self-help method. It began as a moment of union, two minds trying to illuminate the dark.

Let's begin there.

Building the Mirror

When Freud Met Jung

In the winter of 1907, a thirty-one-year-old Swiss psychiatrist boarded a train for Vienna. Carl Gustav Jung, already rising in reputation at the Burghölzli Psychiatric Hospital in Zurich, carried with him a growing admiration for a man he had never met in person, Sigmund Freud. Their correspondence had begun the year prior, when Jung mailed Freud a copy of his *Studies in Word Association*, a paper that impressed Freud immediately. Their intellectual chemistry was undeniable, even through ink and distance.

What began as admiration turned, over the course of thirteen uninterrupted hours, into something deeper: a fusion of minds. Two men, two systems of thought, two vastly different personalities, suddenly aware that they were not alone in their quest to understand the hidden forces that move the human soul. Freud would later describe this moment as historic. Jung would recall it as magnetic. And in that single day, the foundation of modern depth psychology was born.

Before they ever spoke in person, they wrote to each other, volumes, in fact. Their correspondence stretched from 1906 to 1914, revealing both their philosophical kinship and the slow unravelling of their alliance. In one of the earliest letters, Freud expressed his desire for true dialogue, writing: "I am confident that you will often be in a position to back me up, but I shall also gladly accept correction." This wasn't mere flattery. Freud saw in Jung a possible heir to the psychoanalytic tradition he had founded. Jung, for his part, saw in Freud a brilliant pioneer, someone bold enough to claim that the human mind was not fully conscious, and that what we suppress does not disappear.

Their mutual respect was real. But so were the projections.

Freud was the elder, calculated, systematic, and guarded. Jung was the intuitive outsider, open to spiritual ideas, drawn to symbols and myth. On the surface, they agreed about the unconscious. But below that surface, two different worldviews were forming. Still, in those early years, they leaned toward each other. They co-authored the momentum of a movement. Freud began referring patients and analysts to Jung. Jung defended Freud's theories publicly. Together, they established the International Psychoanalytical Association. In 1909, they travelled to Clark University in the United States to deliver lectures on psychoanalysis, introducing the American academic world to their European theories of the mind. Jung even kept a small Freud figurine on his desk.

Yet beneath the collegial warmth, differences simmered.

Where Freud saw the unconscious as a warehouse of repressed instinct, mostly sexual, Jung began to imagine it as something more expansive. He believed the psyche wasn't just shaped by trauma, but also by myth. That dreams didn't just mask forbidden desires; they revealed universal patterns. That healing required not only analysis, but integration. These weren't disagreements. Not yet. But they were signals.

The significance of their alliance goes far beyond the historical. For a time, Freud and Jung reflected the two major poles of the psyche itself: Freud, the rational mind, the realist, the one who says, "Show me the evidence." Jung, the dreaming soul, the seer, the one who whispers, "Look beneath the symbol." Together, they mirrored what every person contains: the instinct to control, and the instinct to become. The fear of chaos, and the draw toward meaning. The need to decode, and the need to trust.

They were, quite literally, building the mirror of the human mind. And it was working, until it wasn't.

Though this book does not begin with their rupture, the seed of it was planted early. Jung once dreamed that he and Freud were excavating a cellar that kept expanding into deeper chambers. Freud, in the dream, refused to go any further. Jung did not stop. It was a dream, yes. But also, a prophecy. One would draw the line at repression. The other would descend into the symbolic, the sacred, the unknowable.

But before that, they believed in each other. Before they split, they built something real. And that's what matters here, because in the evolution of Shadow Work, we must honor its origin. We must acknowledge that, before theory became territory, there was shared courage. Shared imagination. And for a moment, shared purpose.

The Psyche According to Freud

To understand Freud is to begin with structure. He saw the mind not as a mystical space, but as a layered system. Everything had function. Everything had origin. Behaviour was never random, it was the result of forces moving beneath the surface, often without our permission.

Freud's great contribution was not simply the idea of the unconscious. It was that the unconscious *matters*. That what we repress doesn't vanish. It returns, in disguise.

He called this the return of the repressed. And he built a model around it: three parts of the mind working in tension, constantly negotiating the difference between what we want, what we fear, and what we allow ourselves to admit.

The Architecture of the Mind

At the bottom, there was the id, the primal part of us. Pure drive. No morality. No patience. Just hunger, sex, aggression, longing. The id speaks in impulse. It doesn't care about consequences.

Above that sat the ego, the self that must live in the world. The ego is the translator. The realist. It tries to find acceptable ways to meet the id's needs without creating disaster. The ego is who we think we are, most of the time.

And floating above both was the superego, the internalized voice of rules, morality, guilt, and parental commands. It tells us what's right, what's acceptable, and what should never be spoken aloud.

This was Freud's internal trinity. Id, ego, and superego, locked in constant conflict.

And this conflict, he believed, was the root of neurosis.

Repression as Survival

Not everything we feel is allowed. Not everything we think is welcome. So, we push it down. This, Freud believed, is how the unconscious is formed, not as a mystical otherworld, but as a dumping ground for the unacceptable.

We repress what we fear. We repress what we want too much. We repress what might shame us, expose us, or reveal something too raw.

Repression isn't failure. It's protection.

But it comes with a cost. What we repress leaks out. It returns through dreams, symptoms, slips of the tongue, irrational fears, obsessive behaviour. The unconscious doesn't speak in plain language. It speaks in code.

This was Freud's genius. He didn't just point to the mind; he began to decode it.

Desire and the Family Drama

For Freud, repression wasn't random. It had a pattern. He believed the early years of life formed the blueprint for adult behaviour. Not just emotionally, but sexually. His theory of psychosexual development charted a path from oral to anal to phallic stages, each stage forming a piece of the personality.

It was here he introduced the most infamous idea in modern psychology: the Oedipus complex.

Freud claimed that all children pass through a phase where they unconsciously desire the parent of the opposite sex and view the same-sex parent as a rival. This desire is repressed, deeply, and shapes everything that follows: our relationships, our fears, our choice of partners, our anxieties.

To many, this theory felt too specific. Too sexual. Too uncomfortable to be true.

But to Freud, discomfort was evidence. If it made you squirm, it was probably where you needed to look.

The Role of Dreams

Freud believed that dreams were the royal road to the unconscious. In waking life, the ego censors desire. But in dreams, the guard slips. The id sneaks messages through symbolic disguise. A stairway. A tunnel. A locked door. Nothing in a dream is what it seems.

He called this "dream work", the mental process that distorts repressed material so it can appear in dreams without causing panic. The symbols aren't random. They're coded content.

Freud's job was to decode them. And he trained others to do the same.

Shadow as Repression, Not Revelation

If we place Freud's model into the context of Shadow Work, we see something striking. There is no invitation to integrate. There is no sacredness in the shadow. The shadow, in Freud's terms, is a collection of unacceptable drives. To heal is not to reclaim them, but to understand them, to trace them back to their source, and to remove their power through insight and catharsis.

The goal is not to become whole. The goal is to become controlled.

And for many years, this made sense. Freud's framework offered clarity in a time when madness was locked away and trauma was barely spoken of. He named what others wouldn't. He gave language to the dark.

But language is not always enough.

Not every shadow wants to be diagnosed. Some want to be felt. Some want to be seen.

Freud taught us what we fear. But it would take Jung to teach us what we're missing.

The Psyche According to Jung

Jung never set out to replace Freud.

He set out to follow him, deeper, wider, further than Freud was willing to go. For a time, he believed they were walking the same path. But where Freud stopped, Jung stepped into mystery. And from that step, everything changed.

Freud had drawn the mind in three layers: id, ego, and superego, built around repression and desire. Jung didn't argue against that structure. He simply believed it was incomplete. The psyche wasn't just a battlefield of drives and guilt. It was a living system. It didn't just hide things; it longed to become whole.

The Unconscious: Personal and Collective

Jung distinguished between two layers of the unconscious. The first was personal, similar to Freud's idea, made up of repressed memories, forgotten experiences, and suppressed emotion. But beneath that, Jung discovered something far more mysterious: the collective unconscious. This concept, introduced in his 1916 essay *The Structure of the Unconscious*, proposes that all humans inherit a shared psychic substrate composed of archetypes, universal patterns and images that influence our behaviour, perception, and inner life (Jung, *Collected Works*, Vol. 7, §275–280).

Note: The (§) symbol refers to a numbered section from Carl Jung's Collected Works, which are published across multiple volumes. This citation format provides consistency, as page numbers often vary between editions and translations.

This collective layer wasn't individual. It wasn't formed from your childhood or your trauma. It was inherited. Universal. A deep pool of memory and pattern shared across all human beings. Within it lived archetypes, primordial images that shape how we experience the world, long before we have language to name them.

The mother. The hero. The trickster. The wise old man. The shadow. These were not just literary devices or figures of imagination. To Jung, they were living psychic structures. They emerged in dreams, stories, myths, and even the people we are drawn to, or afraid of, without knowing why. As Jung described it: "Archetypes are like riverbeds which dry up when the water deserts them, but which it can find again at any time" (*Man and His Symbols*, 1964, p. 58).

We do not invent archetypes. We remember them.

The Ego and the Self

Jung believed that what we call "I", the ego, is only a fragment of the full self. The ego is necessary. It gives us orientation, decision-making, identity. But it is limited. The **Self**, in Jung's model, is much larger. It includes the conscious and unconscious, light and dark, the parts we accept and the parts we exile. The Self, as defined in *The Relations Between the Ego and the Unconscious* (CW Vol. 7, §274), is the totality of the psyche and the true centre of psychological life.

The process of becoming, that slow unfolding of one's whole being, is what Jung called individuation. It is not perfection. It is not happiness. It is wholeness. And to become whole, we must confront the parts of ourselves we've cast into the dark.

The Shadow

Unlike Freud, who saw the unconscious as a container of unacceptable desires, Jung saw the shadow as everything the ego refuses to identify as "me." The shadow isn't always sinister. Sometimes it's just unfamiliar. Sometimes it's beautiful, qualities we've disowned because they didn't fit the image we were trained to maintain. "The shadow," Jung wrote, "is a moral problem that challenges the whole ego-personality" (*Aion*, CW Vol. 9ii, §13).

But it also holds what we fear. The shadow contains rage, envy, shame, repressed longing, unexpressed grief. The more we deny it, the more it controls us from behind the scenes. "Everyone carries a shadow," Jung famously wrote, "and the less it is embodied in the individual's conscious life, the blacker and denser it is" (*Psychology and Religion*, CW Vol. 11, §131).

To face the shadow is not to fix it. It's to enter relationship with it.

Jung didn't teach repression. He taught recognition.

Dreams and Symbols

In Jung's world, dreams were not distorted wish-fulfillments. They were messages from the deeper self. Not coded lies, but intuitive truths spoken in the language of symbol. "The dream," he wrote, "is a spontaneous self-portrayal, in symbolic form, of the actual situation in the unconscious" (*The Practice of Psychotherapy*, CW Vol. 16, §304).

Symbols, in Jung's theory, aren't decorations. They're bridges. They help the unconscious speak to the conscious mind in a way that bypasses logic and touches knowing.

Jung often advised his patients not to interpret dreams too quickly. Meaning comes, he believed, when the image is lived with. Felt. Honored. When the dream becomes a doorway, not a puzzle.

Active Imagination and Dialogue with the Shadow

Jung introduced a practice he called **active imagination**, a way of engaging directly with unconscious material. Instead of repressing a troubling image or emotion, the individual enters into a conversation with it. They might draw it, write to it, speak to it. They might ask: *What do you want from me? What part of me do you represent?*

This was radical. Not just because it gave value to what Freud dismissed, but because it treated the unconscious not as a threat, but as a guide. "The psychological rule says that when an inner situation is not made conscious, it happens outside, as fate" (*Aion*, CW Vol. 9ii, §126).

The ego, in Jung's system, must relinquish its crown. It must become a listener.

Shadow Work as Integration

Shadow Work, as it is understood today, traces directly back to Jung's concept of individuation. The goal is not to eliminate the shadow. It is to integrate it. To see it, name it, and make space for it in the evolving story of who you are.

This doesn't mean acting out every suppressed desire. It means recognizing that what we hide often holds what we need. That behind the mask of fear is a truth we've waited years to remember.

Jung saw healing not as the end of conflict, but as the acceptance of contradiction. You can be both light and dark. Both confident and insecure. Both rational and intuitive. Integration is the end of pretending, and the beginning of becoming.

He once wrote, "I'd rather be whole than good." That was his ethic. And it is the ethic at the root of Shadow Work.

Freud taught us how to decode the mind., Jung taught us how to listen to the soul.

The Great Divide

The distance between Freud and Jung didn't open suddenly. It stretched gradually, thread by thread, until the cord that had once bound them as mentor and disciple frayed into silence. Their correspondence, once filled with admiration and affirmation, grew clipped. Careful. Then cold. For two men who had once believed they were reshaping the world of the mind, the eventual parting was not just ideological, it was personal.

At the heart of their divide was a single question: What is the source of the psyche's energy?

Freud believed the answer was libido, a sexual energy driving both neurosis and civilization. He held firmly that repressed sexual desires, especially those rooted in early childhood, formed the basis of the unconscious. His model was biologically grounded and culturally controversial. But to Freud, the theory was not moral. It was clinical. To stray from it was to risk losing the clarity of psychoanalysis itself.

Jung, at first, seemed to agree. But as his work deepened, so did his doubts. He began to feel that Freud's insistence on sexuality as the prime mover was reductive. What of dreams that were not erotic? What of visions, myths, spiritual awakenings? Jung saw the psyche as more than a container for impulse. He saw it as a symbolic realm of meaning. Libido, he argued, was not only sexual, but it was also psychic energy, capable of expressing itself in art, religion, love, or suffering. The soul, he believed, had more languages than the body.

The tension came to a head in 1912, with Jung's publication of *Symbols of Transformation* (originally *Wandlungen und Symbole der Libido*). In this pivotal text, Jung reinterpreted libido as a metaphor for broader psychological transformation rather than merely sexual discharge. Freud saw this as a betrayal, a departure from the foundation he had laid. He later remarked that Jung had "lost his grip on reality" and accused him of mystical regression.

Their personal relationship followed suit. Letters became battlegrounds. Jung expressed frustration at Freud's resistance to religious or mythic interpretation. Freud, in turn, accused Jung of heresy. The mentor no longer recognized the student. The student no longer needed the mentor.

Then came the final blow. During a fateful conversation in 1912 in Munich, Freud reportedly fainted in front of Jung. Later, Jung interpreted the incident as symbolic, Freud collapsing under the weight of his own dogma. Freud interpreted it more literally, a stress reaction, perhaps illness. But neither interpretation could patch what had already torn.

By 1913, the break was complete. Jung resigned from the International Psychoanalytical Association. He stepped away not only from Freud but from the movement they had helped shape together. It was a risk. Freud had the audience, the influence, the following. Jung had only his intuition, and a growing collection of dreams, symbols, and stories.

He chose to follow them.

For the next few years, Jung entered what he called his "confrontation with the unconscious." In solitude, he began writing, drawing, dreaming, not for science, but for survival. This deeply personal descent would become the basis for his *Red Book*, a private exploration of soul and symbol that he kept hidden for decades. It was here, not in textbooks or conferences, that the true genesis of Shadow Work began.

While Freud continued to refine his structural model and clinical applications, Jung walked into a darker, stranger terrain. He saw the unconscious not as a chamber of shame but as a field of potential, fertile, frightening, alive. And it was there, in that unseen territory, that the idea of the shadow would take root.

Their split wasn't simply a philosophical disagreement. It was a rupture between two worldviews: one that believed the human mind must be controlled and decoded, and another that believed the soul must be revealed and reclaimed.

They never reconciled.

Yet in their fracture, a new lens emerged, one that would influence therapy, spirituality, art, literature, trauma recovery, and inner healing for generations to come.

Shadow Work was born not from harmony, but from tension. Not from agreement, but from departure. And it is in that space, between fear and freedom, that the shadow still speaks.

The Birth of the Shadow

The idea of the shadow was not born in a laboratory or clinic. It emerged from solitude, from ink-stained pages, from Jung's descent into what he later called his "confrontation with the unconscious." After the break with Freud, Jung did not immediately launch a new school of psychology. He withdrew. He listened. He wrote. Between 1913 and 1917, Jung documented dreams, visions, drawings, and inner dialogues in what would later be published as *The Red Book*. He called it "a more or less voluntary confrontation with the unconscious." What he found in that confrontation was not only chaos, but clarity.

The psyche, as Jung began to map it, was not merely a stage for repression. It was a dynamic system of symbols, each representing some part of the whole self. But the conscious ego, he saw, could never hold the totality of that system. It was too limited, too fragile. And so, everything the ego could not or would not identify as "me" was pushed aside. That cast-off portion, rejected, forgotten, denied, was the beginning of what Jung called *the shadow*.

The shadow was not a flaw. It was a function. It preserved what was not yet ready to be known. It protected the self from collapse by holding contradiction in the dark. But over time, the shadow gained mass. It gathered resentment, grief, longing, rage. It became, in Jung's words, "a moral problem that challenges the whole ego-personality." (Jung, *Aion*, CW Vol. 9ii, §13).

Unlike Freud, who placed emphasis on instinctual drives, primarily sexual, Jung came to view psychic energy as symbolic. He did not deny the existence of biological instincts. But he felt they pointed to something deeper: the need for integration, for inner unity. The shadow was not simply a container of forbidden desires; it was the place where all undeveloped potential lived. Strength not claimed. Courage never embodied. Love buried under shame.

The personal shadow forms early. A child who is punished for anger learns to repress assertiveness. A girl told not to "brag" hides her confidence. A boy told "boys don't cry" buries his grief and grows a mask. As social identity takes shape, anything that threatens belonging is sent underground. The shadow becomes not just a storehouse of what is wrong, but of what is missing.

Jung's theory expanded the scope of psychological healing. Where Freud had focused on uncovering the source of neurosis, Jung proposed a deeper aim: integration. To become whole, one had to meet the self in all its aspects, including the ones most feared. Dreams, he said, were the unconscious attempting to restore balance. Symbols offered the bridge. And the shadow was the first threshold.

Jung never offered a step-by-step guide to shadow work. He believed the process was archetypal but also deeply personal. It could begin in therapy, but it could just as easily begin in a dream, a relationship, a breakdown, or a creative act. What mattered was the willingness to *see*, to look at what had long been avoided. "Knowing your own darkness," he wrote, "is the best method for dealing with the darknesses of other people."

He did not romanticize this process. The shadow, when met, is not friendly. It does not speak in polite sentences. It appears in projection, when we despise in others what we refuse to acknowledge in ourselves. It appears in sabotage, when our repeated patterns defy our conscious desires. It appears in rage, jealousy, contempt, withdrawal, addiction, obsession, shame. Not because we are broken, but because we are split.

Shadow work, then, is not the excavation of trauma. It is the integration of truth.

Jung's psychological model offered the first true invitation to this work. His structure was circular, not linear. The Self was not the ego, but the whole psyche, and the journey toward it was one of deepening awareness, not achievement. The goal was not to "fix" the parts of us that didn't fit our self-image, but to reclaim them. To bring light to what was lost, not to erase it.

He introduced the idea of *active imagination*, a method of dialoguing with inner figures through writing, drawing, even speaking aloud. He encouraged not the analysis of symbols, but the *experience* of them. What does the angry figure in the dream want from you? What does the neglected child inside your psyche need to say? The shadow is not a puzzle to solve. It is a relationship to enter. *(link.springer.com, en.wikipedia.org)*

In this way, Jung laid the foundation for what would become a global practice. Shadow work in its contemporary form, found in therapy, self-help, spirituality, somatic healing, even TikTok psychology, has its roots here. Not in perfection, but in paradox. Not in diagnosis, but in dialogue. The shadow is not your enemy. It is the part of you that waited to be invited back.

And like all long-lost parts, it carries both pain and promise.

From Myth to Method

Jung never believed psychology should be confined to the observable. The mind, he argued, was not merely a mechanism of reactions but a symbolic realm. And so he stepped beyond clinical science into a language many psychologists feared: myth. He did not see this as a regression into superstition but an evolution toward deeper understanding. "Myths are original revelations of the pre-conscious psyche," he wrote, "involuntary statements about unconscious psychic happenings" (*Symbols of Transformation*, CW Vol. 5, §652). It was not the literal content of myth that mattered, it was the psychic truth encoded within it.

This move widened the rift between Jung and Freud. In a letter from March 3, 1910, Jung responded to Freud's discomfort with his increasing focus on spiritual symbolism. Freud, wary of mysticism, had warned him that "the further you go into the symbolic, the less you remain scientific." Jung replied, "I cannot sacrifice the numinous. For me, these images are not detours from science, they are the language of the psyche itself." The split, though not yet formalized, was growing.

Where Freud analysed dreams for repressed wishes, Jung listened for the voice of the unconscious attempting to correct the conscious imbalance. A snake was not just a phallic symbol; it could be the archetype of transformation. A flood in a dream was not simply a memory of trauma, but a sign of psychic renewal. These were not projections of past events but invitations from deeper structures: archetypes, universal motifs that emerged across time and culture, encoded in what Jung called the *collective unconscious*.

To Jung, shadow work was not just introspection, it was myth enacted. The hero's journey was no longer a story reserved for literature; it became a psychological map. In myth, the hero is called to descend into the underworld, to meet the beast, the witch, the wounded king. This descent, Jung saw, was symbolic of the confrontation with the shadow. The underworld was the unconscious. The beast, one's repressed desire. The witch, a projection of the wounded feminine. The wounded king, a reflection of the broken authority within. The task was not to kill the monster, but to recognize it as a lost part of oneself.

This symbolic structure became the foundation for what Jung called *individuation*, the lifelong process of integrating unconscious material into conscious awareness. "Individuation means becoming an 'individual,'" he wrote, "and, in so far as 'individuality' embraces our innermost, last, and incomparable uniqueness, it also implies becoming one's own self" (*Two Essays on Analytical Psychology*, CW Vol. 7, §266). This was no short journey. It was not therapy in the modern sense but soul-work, a method of psychological alchemy.

The tools he developed were not prescriptive formulas, but invitations to inner dialogue. *Active imagination*, his term for engaging with images and voices from the unconscious, was one such method. Rather than analyse a dream figure to death, Jung asked: What would it say if you spoke to it? What would happen if you followed it, painted it, gave it a voice?

This was not fantasy. This was encounter. As he described in *The Red Book*, "I had to realize that I had lost my soul... therefore I took it back from the spirit of the times and ventured into the depths" (*The Red Book*, 2009, p. 229). In this inner world, Jung met

Philemon, an archetypal figure who became his inner teacher. He did not call this hallucination. He called it revelation.

The shadow, in this framework, was not limited to the personal. It existed at every layer, individual, cultural, collective. A man might project his unacknowledged anger onto his colleague. A nation might scapegoat a minority to avoid its own failings. A culture might romanticize the light and suppress the dark. Jung warned: "The brighter the light, the darker the shadow."

In one of his later reflections on the early split with Freud, Jung confessed that his friend had been right to fear the unconscious, but wrong to limit it. "Freud had discovered a basement," he said, "but I suspected there were still deeper levels." These deeper levels were not simply pathological, they were mythic, symbolic, and sacred.

In the years that followed, Jung's method, dream analysis, symbol amplification, active imagination, and archetypal exploration, formed the pillars of what many now call shadow work. But he never claimed to invent it. "The shadow is a living part of the personality," he wrote, "and therefore wants to live with it in some form." It cannot be cut away. It must be met, heard, integrated.

What he offered was a method, not to solve the shadow, but to live with it consciously. In doing so, we recover more than what we lost. We recover the story of who we truly are, behind the mask. Myth becomes method. And method, if honored with humility, becomes transformation.

Projection and Pain

The Mirror of Others

The shadow does not hide in caves. It walks with us. It sits beside us at dinner. It enters every relationship we form and every judgment we pass. Jung observed that what is hidden within us inevitably seeks expression, not always through conscious action, but often through projection. "Everything that irritates us about others," he wrote, "can lead us to an understanding of ourselves" (*The Practice of Psychotherapy*, CW Vol. 16, §285).

Projection is not mere dislike. It is the unconscious transference of our disowned qualities onto others. It's the anger we deny in ourselves that we see in the short temper of a friend. The ambition we repress that we resent in a colleague. The shame we bury that we ridicule in someone else's vulnerability. The shadow knows no boundaries, it will wear any mask, use any relationship, take any opportunity to make itself visible.

In a 1911 letter to Freud, Jung confessed his growing awareness that repression was not just intrapsychic, it was relational. "I sense that we exile much of our own pain into the people closest to us," he wrote. "How else to explain the clarity with which we recognize their flaws, but none of our own?" Freud replied with clinical detachment, suggesting that this was a neurotic symptom, not a psychological structure. But Jung saw something more enduring. Projection, to him, was not a pathology, it was a mirror.

Nowhere is this more apparent than in intimate relationships. The people we fall for, fight with, or flee from are often shadow carriers. They hold what we long for and fear most. A man may be drawn to a woman's warmth, only to resent her emotional intensity. A woman may idolize her partner's ambition, only to later accuse him of selfishness. What begins in attraction often devolves into frustration, not because the other has changed, but because the shadow has surfaced.

Jung wrote extensively about *anima* and *animus*, the inner feminine in men and the inner masculine in women, not as gendered clichés but as archetypes of psychological polarity.

When undeveloped, these inner figures are projected onto romantic partners. The partner becomes an ideal, a saviour, or an enemy, not for who they are, but for what they represent within the unconscious of the lover. "The meeting of two personalities," Jung said, "is like the contact of two chemical substances: if there is any reaction, both are transformed" (*Modern Man in Search of a Soul*, 1933).

Projection is not limited to lovers. We project onto parents, children, friends, strangers. Entire social groups are scapegoated for what a culture cannot face. Racism, sexism, homophobia, nationalism, each carries the fingerprints of collective shadow. What is feared or despised within is externalized. As Jung warned in *The Undiscovered Self*, "The mass man is most dangerous when he imagines himself to be virtuous."

The pain of projection is its blindness. We do not know we are doing it. The angry partner believes their rage is justified. The jealous friend insists they are only being cautious. The prejudiced mind cloaks its fear in tradition. But the effect is the same: the other becomes the vessel for what the self refuses to hold. And thus, the work begins, not in changing the other, but in reclaiming the projection.

This is the heart of shadow work in relational life. To pause in judgment and ask: What part of me is speaking here? What emotion am I trying not to feel? What wound is being touched by this moment? These are not easy questions. They require humility, self-inquiry, and emotional courage. But they are the doorway back to integrity.

In therapeutic settings, projection is often where breakthroughs occur. The client blames a parent, a partner, a boss. The therapist gently reflects. Over time, the pattern reveals itself. The enemy shrinks. The self expands. And the shadow, when seen with compassion, no longer needs a scapegoat.

But the danger of projection does not end with awareness. As Jung cautioned, "One does not become enlightened by imagining figures of light, but by making the darkness conscious." Merely noticing projection is not enough. One must trace its origin, feel its roots, and integrate the energy it carries.

Harry, our fictional case, was a man driven by longing and shaped by wounds. After two failed marriages and a string of hollow relationships, he entered therapy convinced that women could not be trusted.

But as his sessions deepened, he began to notice a pattern. Each partner had mirrored his own emotional hunger, his fear of abandonment, and his unmet childhood needs. What he had projected as betrayal was, in part, a replay of his own vulnerability. Slowly, painfully, he began to reclaim the pieces of himself he had tried to outsource.

The process was not linear. It rarely is. He had to grieve the illusion. He had to sit in the discomfort of his own projections. But in doing so, he no longer needed his ex-partners to be monsters or angels. They became human. And so did he.

The mirror of the other, when used consciously, becomes a portal to the self. Projection ceases to be a trap and becomes a teacher. And in that shift, shadow work moves out of theory and into the very fabric of everyday life.

The Rise of Integration

From Inner Division to Wholeness

Integration was never Jung's end goal for the sake of harmony alone. It was the culmination of a lifelong psychological movement toward authenticity, the merging of conscious and unconscious forces into what he termed the Self. To understand how integration became the central pillar of Jungian shadow work, we must first revisit the crisis that made it necessary. The Great Divide, the philosophical split from Freud, was more than an ideological rift. It was the symbolic fracture of Western psychology into two opposing worldviews: one rooted in reductionism, the other in meaning.

For Freud, the psyche was the battleground of suppressed desires and primitive drives. Healing, then, was the unveiling of the hidden cause, a return to the scene of repression. But for Jung, healing could not stop at exposure. He believed the psyche was not only a site of conflict, but also a field of potential. His was a psychology of *becoming*, not merely remembering.

After breaking from Freud, Jung entered what he called his "confrontation with the unconscious." During this time, he experienced a series of waking visions, spontaneous drawings, and dialogues with inner figures. What emerged was not insanity, but insight.

Through this descent, he mapped the structures of the psyche: the ego, the personal unconscious, the collective unconscious, and the archetypes. Integration, in this map, was the process by which the fragmented ego gradually encountered, dialogued with, and eventually incorporated these deeper elements.

But this was no simple task.

The path of integration meant stepping into paradox. It meant recognizing that what we fear in others' lives in us. It meant seeing that dreams are not random, but coded invitations. It meant accepting that the unconscious was not just a container for trauma, but a source of wisdom. Jung saw the psyche as a self-regulating system. When we veer too far from our inner truth, symptoms arise not merely as dysfunction, but as messages. Depression may be the soul's plea for descent. Anxiety, a signal of inner dissonance. Projection, a cry from the shadow for recognition.

The rise of integration as a therapeutic model gained traction slowly. In the decades following Jung's most prolific work, his ideas were overshadowed in clinical psychology by more measurable methods: behaviourism, cognitive restructuring, and medical psychiatry. Yet quietly, his concepts filtered into broader domains. Artists, philosophers, mystics, and trauma theorists began to find in his work a psychological language that mirrored the mythic journey of the soul.

The individuation process, Jung's term for the full arc of integration, was a radical reframe. It suggested that life was not a linear ascent toward social success, but a spiral of descent and return. One descends into the unknown, into dreams, memories, projections, and disowned parts of the self. And then, with new awareness, one returns, changed, expanded, whole. This idea paralleled ancient initiatory rites: the descent into the underworld, the night sea journey, the alchemical transformation.

In fact, Jung's *Mysterium Coniunctionis* was an entire treatise on the alchemical symbolism of psychological integration. He drew direct parallels between the union of opposites in alchemy, sun and moon, masculine and feminine, spirit and matter, and the union of the ego with the unconscious. The goal of therapy was not to become perfect, but to become whole. "I would rather be whole than good," Jung famously said.

This notion opened a new vista: Spiritual integration.

Unlike Freud, who dismissed religion as neurosis, Jung saw spirituality as a legitimate expression of the psyche. He spoke of God not as a theological figure, but as an archetypal presence. In dreams, visions, and numinous experiences, individuals often encountered the divine not through doctrine, but through inner symbols. For Jung, integration included this dimension. To deny the spiritual instinct was to repress an essential function of human wholeness.

Modern psychology, particularly in transpersonal and depth modalities, owes much to this vision. Somatic therapies, internal family systems, dreamwork, narrative therapy, and archetypal coaching all draw on Jung's scaffolding, even when unacknowledged. The language of the inner child, the saboteur, the exile, all are echoes of shadow archetypes. Integration today is no longer confined to Jungian clinics. It lives in coaching circles, trauma-informed spaces, breathwork ceremonies, and creative healing arts.

Yet the process remains elusive. Integration is not the same as insight. Knowing your shadow does not mean you have made peace with it. The intellect can grasp what the heart has not yet metabolized. Thus, the work must be embodied. For Jung, symbols were not abstract ideas, they were felt realities. A person must not only understand the symbol but enter into relationship with it. This is where the alchemical metaphor becomes vital. The work is not quick. It requires heat, pressure, and time.

The integration of opposites, light and dark, masculine and feminine, ego and Self, is never finished. It is an ongoing dance. Jung warned against the premature assumption of wholeness. To claim enlightenment while the shadow remains unconscious is spiritual inflation. Integration is not arrival. It is practice. One does not become whole once. One becomes whole again and again, in each moment of conscious choice.

Perhaps most strikingly, integration demands humility. To look within and admit that you have hated, envied, manipulated, feared, abandoned, and betrayed, not just been a victim, but also an agent, requires the death of self-image. But it is precisely in that death that something more authentic can be born. As Jung wrote, "The privilege of a lifetime is to become who you truly are."

Integration in the 21st Century: The Return of the Soul

In today's therapeutic landscape, Jung's legacy finds new life in emerging modalities that honor the complexity of the human psyche. The term "shadow work" now appears in online courses, social media posts, and even wellness marketing campaigns. But beneath the commodification lies a genuine hunger for depth. In an age dominated by speed, stimulation, and surface-level connection, the idea of integrating the rejected, hidden, and unconscious parts of the self has gained profound relevance.

Practices such as Internal Family Systems (IFS), developed by Richard Schwartz, echo Jung's archetypal inner dialogues. IFS speaks of inner parts, wounded exiles, protective managers, and firefighter roles, all psychological stand-ins for the cast of inner characters Jung explored through active imagination and dream analysis. These parts represent elements of the shadow that, when given space to speak, begin to soften, heal, and integrate.

Similarly, somatic-based therapies like Peter Levine's Somatic Experiencing address the body as a site of memory, story, and symbolic trauma. Jung had already noted that the unconscious is not merely a psychological construct, it lives in the flesh. Today's trauma modalities validate that the body holds what the mind forgets. Breathwork, sound healing, yoga, and expressive movement are now embraced as avenues for symbolic reintegration.

Digital spaces have also become unlikely hosts for shadow integration. Influencers and therapists alike now teach shadow work through video platforms, guided meditations, and virtual retreats. While not all are rooted in rigorous psychological training, the interest reveals something telling: people are no longer content with surface solutions. There is a collective yearning for emotional depth, soul integrity, and personal meaning. Jung anticipated this. "People will do anything, no matter how absurd," he wrote, "to avoid facing their own souls."

Yet something has shifted. A new generation, disillusioned by systems that prize productivity over presence, is beginning to turn inward, not in withdrawal, but in reclamation. Collective trauma events such as the *COVID-19* pandemic, widespread ecological anxiety, and social injustice movements have awakened a need to process not only the personal shadow but also the communal one. Shadow work is now becoming a language of cultural repair.

Therapists increasingly blend Jungian theory with mindfulness, indigenous wisdom traditions, and storytelling as a healing tool. This intersection, psychology meeting myth, science meeting soul, marks a return to a more holistic psychology. It is no longer enough to reduce pain to pathology. Integration honors pain as a teacher. As Jung asserted, "There is no coming to consciousness without pain."

This rising wave of inner work does not abandon Freud's contributions, but it transcends them. Where Freud explored the basement of the psyche, Jung pointed toward the sky as well. The future of shadow work belongs to those who can walk both below and above, who can grieve their fragmentation while still imagining their integration.

In this rising call to integration, we rediscover what Jung tried to tell us all along: the soul is not something to be fixed, it is something to be remembered, honored, and made whole.

The Archetypes Within

Mapping the Inner Mythology

Long before modern psychology began mapping the mind, humanity was already dreaming in symbols. From ancient myths and sacred stories to the recurring figures that populate our dreams, there has always been a deeper language at work, one that speaks not in words, but in images. Carl Gustav Jung gave this phenomenon a name: archetypes. But even that term is merely a gateway into a much older understanding of the psyche. These inner patterns, or symbolic blueprints, form the architecture of our inner world, shaping how we see ourselves, others, and the journey of life itself.

Jung did not invent the idea of universal psychic structures. He observed them. Across cultures, continents, and millennia, he noticed recurring figures emerging in stories, dreams, and visions: the wise old man, the nurturing mother, the devouring shadow, the heroic child, the elusive trickster. He called them archetypes, borrowing from Plato's notion of ideal forms. But unlike Plato's abstract models, Jung's figures were living, breathing elements of the unconscious, primordial images that carried emotional weight and psychic energy.

To encounter these figures is to enter the mythic dimension of the psyche. One does not merely analyse a dream about being chased; one meets the archetype of the Predator or the Fear Bearer. One does not simply feel drawn to a romantic partner; one projects the Anima or Animus, the inner feminine or masculine, onto the beloved. These figures live within us, but they appear to us as if from outside. In this way, archetypes are not just patterns; they are the symbols through which the unconscious speaks.

Jung identified several foundational archetypes, though he never claimed to offer a complete list. Among the most significant were:

- **The Shadow**: the repressed, denied, or feared parts of ourselves. The Shadow often appears in dreams as a threatening figure, a rival, or even a monster. But its purpose is not to destroy, it seeks integration.

- **The Anima/Animus**: the inner opposite gender. For a man, the Anima represents his inner feminine. For a woman, the Animus is her inner masculine. These inner counterparts guide emotional balance and relational depth.

- **The Persona**: the social mask. This is the role we play in public, shaped by cultural expectation and ego adaptation. The danger is mistaking the mask for the self.

- **The Self**: the totality of the psyche. Not to be confused with the ego, the Self is the integrating centre that harmonizes all parts of the inner system. It is both the goal and the guide of individuation.

- **The Wise Old Man/Woman**: the inner guide, often appearing as a sage, elder, healer, or seer in dreams and stories.

- **The Trickster**: the disruptor of order. Mischievous, unpredictable, and often irreverent, this figure breaks the rules to reveal deeper truths.

- **The Divine Child**: symbol of renewal, innocence, and future potential. Often emerging in times of despair or loss, it signifies rebirth.

These psychic figures do not live in isolation. They interact, overlap, and evolve across the landscape of the unconscious. They form what could be called a personal mythology: a unique constellation of symbolic roles that replay themselves in our inner dramas, external relationships, and lifelong patterns.

Freud, by contrast, constructed a more linear and functionalist model of the mind: the id, the ego, and the superego. For Freud, the psyche was primarily the stage for internal conflict between instinctual drives, reality constraints, and moral judgment. While he acknowledged fantasy, he viewed dreams and projections as distortions of repressed desire, not as symbolic messages from a larger self. His model was analytical, diagnostic, and biologically grounded.

Jung's framework moved in a different direction, toward meaning, mystery, and myth. He proposed that within each person lies a collective unconscious, populated by these recurring symbolic figures. They are not learned; they are inherited. Much like the instincts of animals, these patterns shape behaviour before experience fills them with content. You do not learn to fear abandonment; you come into the world with a psychic mold shaped by generations of loss. The specific story may be yours, but the underlying structure is shared.

In this way, the archetypal lens is both personal and transpersonal. Your mother may have her own name, history, and personality, but within you, she also activates the Mother figure, nurturing or devouring, healing or abandoning. Your partner may be entirely unique, but the projections you place upon them arise from the Anima or Animus. Understanding these patterns allows for deeper self-awareness and more compassionate relationships.

Jung's method of *active imagination* became a key practice for engaging these inner figures. By dialoguing with the symbols and characters that arise in dreams or fantasies, a person could access deeper insights into their own inner landscape. The goal was not to silence these voices, but to listen, to allow the unconscious to speak in its own language. In doing so, healing becomes a conversation, not a conquest.

Throughout his life, Jung applied this symbolic framework to literature, alchemy, art, religion, and even politics. He saw in Goethe's *Faust*, in Dante's *Divine Comedy*, in the visions of mystics and the rituals of indigenous cultures, the same figures and storylines repeating. Not because they were copied, but because they arose from the same collective psychic ground. In Jung's view, every culture dreamed its way into meaning. And every individual, too, must navigate their own symbolic labyrinth.

The modern era has not diminished these patterns. In fact, contemporary films, novels, and television series are arguably the new mythology. Characters like Darth Vader, Neo, Elsa, or the Joker are not merely fictional, they are expressions of the Shadow, the Chosen One, the Ice Queen, the Trickster. Audiences resonate with these figures not because they are new, but because they are familiar. They speak to the deep psyche. They wear new clothes but carry ancient energy.

In therapy, the recognition of these inner characters can be transformative. A client may speak of their critical inner voice, not realizing they are contending with a harsh Superego or an internalized Punisher. Another may dream of a lost child, not knowing this figure symbolizes a neglected emotional self. When these figures are brought into conscious dialogue, they begin to shift. Healing begins not with elimination, but with relationship.

In the second half of life, what Jung called the *afternoon of life*, the work of individuation becomes more urgent. The archetypes no longer stay quiet in the basement. They emerge, sometimes with force. Midlife crises, spiritual awakenings, breakdowns, and breakthroughs are often the psyche's demand to pay attention to neglected parts. What was once repressed becomes active. The Shadow knocks louder. The Self begins to pull us inward.

In the next section, we will explore how these patterns operate within contemporary therapeutic and creative frameworks, showing not only how to recognize them, but how to work with them as allies in the journey of integration.

Therapeutic Integration and Creative Alchemy

The recognition and engagement of inner symbols has become foundational in many modern therapeutic modalities. Depth psychologists, Jungian analysts, and trauma-informed practitioners all draw from this archetypal lens to help individuals encounter the unconscious with curiosity rather than fear. In Internal Family Systems (IFS), for example, the psyche is seen as composed of "parts", some protective, some wounded, some wise. Though not named as such, these parts often mirror the roles described by Jung. A critical voice might be a distorted Persona; a protector might be the Warrior or the Judge; a young emotional wound might take the form of the Inner Child or Orphan.

Modern dream analysis has also moved from reductionist interpretations to symbolic unfolding. Therapists often invite clients to re-enter their dreams imaginatively, dialoguing with dream figures or re-envisioning endings. Rather than decoding dreams as secret messages, the aim is to explore them as spontaneous myths produced by the unconscious. In this space, every symbol matters, and each figure offers a mirror to some part of the self.

Art therapy and expressive writing also serve as vessels for engaging these inner forms. When individuals create images, tell stories, or move intuitively, they bypass the linear mind and access what Jung called the "symbol-producing function" of the psyche.

A painted mask may reveal a hidden Persona; a poem may voice the Anima's longing; a sculpture may externalize the Shadow. In these moments, creativity becomes alchemy, the transformation of psychic material into visible, felt, and movable form.

Jung wrote extensively about this process, noting in *The Red Book* that the soul speaks in images. In one passage, he reflects, "The images of the unconscious place a great responsibility upon a man. Failure to understand them, or a shrinking from them, deprives him of his wholeness and imposes a painful fragmentariness on his life." The act of turning toward these images, even when difficult, allows for healing that is deeper than diagnosis. It allows for the kind of growth that is not about self-improvement, but self-reclamation.

Contemporary shadow work practitioners, coaches, and spiritual guides have expanded this approach beyond therapy into holistic, somatic, and digital spaces. Guided meditations, inner child healing, shadow mapping exercises, and archetype embodiment rituals now proliferate on platforms from YouTube to wellness retreats. Some purists argue this dilutes Jung's original framework, while others suggest it signifies the very thing Jung predicted, that his ideas would evolve into a new mythology suited for the modern soul.

The truth may lie somewhere in between. What remains essential is that individuals begin to recognize their own patterns, not just intellectually, but emotionally and symbolically. When someone sees their repetitive conflict with authority figures as a reenactment of the Father Wound or discovers that their people-pleasing is a form of Shadow avoidance, they move from reaction to reflection. This shift opens the door to change not through willpower, but through insight.

In working with clients or reflecting on our own lives, the question becomes: What inner figure is asking to be seen? Who have I cast out or idolized? What part of me is masquerading as someone else's expectation? And, most vitally, what story am I living that is not mine to carry?

These questions do not lead to tidy answers. They lead us deeper, into the mythic undercurrents of our personal histories. The archetypal journey is not about arriving at perfection but about returning to authenticity. It is about honoring the cast of inner characters not as flaws to fix, but as voices to understand.

In the final section of this chapter, we'll look at how these symbolic figures shape not just individuals, but collective narratives, especially in times of upheaval, cultural transition, and spiritual emergence.

Cultural Mirrors and Collective Shadows

The symbolic figures that shape our personal lives do not stop at the boundary of the individual psyche, they scale upward, taking form in the myths of nations, the ethos of generations, and the collective movements that sweep through societies. Jung often warned that what we fail to integrate personally will inevitably erupt collectively. When a culture refuses to look at its shadow, it will project it outward, onto other races, other ideologies, other nations.

The archetypal forces that animate an individual can also possess a group. The Hero can become the fanatic. The Victim can fuel resentment. The Orphan may become a collective cry for belonging. When left unconscious, these patterns shape revolutions, wars, cultural renaissances, and societal collapses. We see them in the scapegoating of minorities, in the romanticizing of past empires, in the demonization of the unknown. As Jung wrote in 1946, in the wake of World War II, "The gigantic catastrophes that threaten us today are not elemental happenings of a physical or biological order but are psychic events."

In times of upheaval, climate anxiety, pandemics, political extremism, economic collapse, the symbols shift. The Trickster appears more frequently, disguised in satire or chaos. The Warrior may resurface in both its distorted and noble forms. The Wise Elder is often absent, highlighting our culture's neglect of true mentorship. And the Child, the hope for a future not yet written, appears ever more fragile and in need of protection.

Popular media has become a stage for these dynamics. The rise of dystopian fiction, superhero sagas, and mythic antiheroes reflects a culture wrestling with complexity. Characters like Black Panther, Katniss Everdeen, the Joker, and Eleven are not simply entertainment, they are mirrors of our collective state. They reveal our longings, our unhealed wounds, our unspoken fears, and our latent potential.

Modern movements, such as #MeToo, Black Lives Matter, climate activism, and digital sovereignty, also tap into symbolic narratives. Each carries archetypal energies: the Rebel, the Truth-Teller, the Exile, the Healer. Their power lies not just in political demand, but in their mythic resonance. They stir something ancient in us, the need for justice, belonging, dignity, and transformation.

Jung foresaw this interplay between psyche and civilization. He believed that every cultural crisis is also a spiritual one. When a society loses its myth, it loses its direction. And when its people cannot face their own shadows, they fall prey to collective possession. Healing, then, is not only personal. It is also political, cultural, and mythic.

In this era, shadow work has become more than a psychological practice, it has become a necessary collective act. To do our inner work is no longer a luxury. It is a responsibility. It is the means by which we resist repetition and create new stories.

Jung once wrote, "Who looks outside, dreams, who looks inside, awakes." But today, we must do both. We must awaken to the symbolic forces within while remaining alert to the dream being enacted around us. Only then can we become conscious participants in the unfolding myth of our time.

Beyond the Shadow

The Return to the Self

The Concept of the Self in Jungian Psychology

Jung's notion of the Self is not to be mistaken for the everyday self, our roles, personalities, or ego identities. Rather, the Self represents the totality of the psyche: conscious and unconscious, known and unknown, fragmented and integrated. It is both the source and the goal of psychological development. The Self is not something we construct, but something we gradually remember, a buried wholeness beneath the rubble of adaptation and defence.

Unlike Freud, who saw the ego as the arbiter between instinct and society, Jung viewed the ego as merely one aspect of a much larger psychic system. For Jung, the ego is like a candle; the Self is the sun. The Self contains all potential: shadow and light, male and female, trauma and transcendence. To discover the Self is not to become perfect, but to become whole.

Jung believed the Self communicates with us through symbols, dreams, synchronicities, and deep emotional stirrings. It pulls us toward experiences that challenge our current identity so that deeper truths can be unveiled. In his writings, Jung described this process not as linear, but as circular or spiral, an alchemical unfolding. We are drawn repeatedly into experiences that dissolve the old structures, so something truer can emerge.

In dreams, the Self may appear as a wise old man, a divine child, a mandala, or even a landscape. In real life, it may show up as a life crisis, a profound loss, or an unexpected longing that refuses to be silenced. The Self is not simply who we are, it is who we are meant to become when we stop living from fear or imitation.

The Self cannot be possessed. It must be lived into. And every time we make a decision that honors inner truth over social script, we come closer to its centre. That is the quiet miracle of individuation: not to become someone else, but to finally come home to who we already are.

Individuation as a Life Journey

Individuation is the process by which a person becomes a psychological "individual," a separate, indivisible unity or "whole." It is not a goal to be ticked off a list but a deepening journey into one's essence, a dialogue between the conscious self and the unconscious depths. Jung believed that without this process, we remain fragmented, overly identified with persona, and driven by unconscious complexes that control our behaviour from the shadows.

At the heart of individuation is the integration of opposites: reason and feeling, strength and vulnerability, instinct and intellect. Rather than trying to resolve these in favour of one side, Jung taught us to hold the tension, to let the psyche metabolize these polarities into a third, transcendent function. This inner synthesis becomes the seed of personal transformation.

The journey often begins with a crisis, a moment when the ego can no longer maintain its illusion of control. A failed marriage, the loss of a parent, the collapse of a belief system, burnout, addiction, or simply an unbearable sense of meaninglessness can all act as catalysts. These breakdowns, rather than being signs of weakness, are invitations from the psyche to go deeper.

Throughout this journey, the ego is slowly decentred. The goal is not ego death, but ego flexibility. One learns to relate to inner voices rather than be ruled by them. Dreams become guideposts. Synchronicities begin to surface, nudging us toward teachers, books, places, and people that stir something ancient and unfinished within us.

A crucial phase of individuation involves engaging the Shadow, not just intellectually, but emotionally. This means feeling grief, rage, jealousy, terror, and shame without being consumed by them. It requires us to own projections, make amends, and take radical responsibility for what lives in our psychic basement.

Beyond the Shadow lies deeper territory: the encounter with the Anima or Animus, the inner feminine or masculine image that shapes our relationships and creative life. Jung believed this stage opens access to the symbolic imagination, a richer perception of reality that transcends logic. When these inner figures are integrated, we become less reactive, more intuitive, more whole.

The final movement of individuation is the emergence of the Self, not as a static identity, but as a living centre that orients the psyche toward integrity. This phase is marked not by perfection, but by a growing capacity to live in alignment with one's inner truth despite external pressures. It is not about becoming someone else, it is about becoming real.

Jung described individuation as "the adventure of the soul." It is lonely at times, because few choose to walk this path. But it is also luminous, because each layer of healing brings us closer to the truth that we are not broken, only buried.

Letters and Writings on the Self

Jung's own writings on the Self are some of the most poetic and spiritually resonant in the history of psychology. In *Memories, Dreams, Reflections*, he described the Self as "a God-image," not in the sense of divinity imposed from above, but as a sacred centre within each human life. He wrote of his own inner experiences as encounters with something vast and numinous, beyond intellect yet deeply personal.

In his correspondence, Jung often returned to the theme of individuation. In a 1959 letter to Victor White, Jung wrote, "I do not hold myself to be a Christian in the conventional sense, but I do believe that the experience of the Self is the experience of God." Here, Jung was elevating psychological wholeness into the realm of spiritual encounter, a radical stance that positioned the human psyche as the true temple of transformation.

Another powerful letter, written to a colleague in 1945, stated: "The goal of psychological development is the self-realization of the whole man, that is, individuation or becoming whole." This line echoed his clinical observations and personal convictions: that healing was not about fixing symptoms but about aligning with one's deeper truth.

In *Aion*, one of his major works on the Self, Jung laid out the psychological and symbolic dimensions of the ego-Self axis. He explored the way symbols like the mandala represented the structure of the Self, and how myths and religious images carried deep psychological meaning. Jung argued that the Self does not merely emerge, it constellates, forms, and reveals itself through our deepest inner work.

These writings form the backbone of modern understanding around the concept of inner wholeness. They suggest that healing is not merely about comfort, it is about consciousness. And the

Self is not a fantasy, but a sacred potential woven into the very architecture of our psyche.

Modern Interpretations and Misunderstandings

In today's digital age, the concept of the Self has taken on both new significance and widespread distortion. The word "Self" is often misused as a synonym for the ego or individual personality, stripped of its Jungian depth and symbolic nuance. Social media platforms encourage a curated identity, where authenticity is often overshadowed by performance. As a result, many mistake the quest for followers and external validation for true self-realization.

The language of "finding yourself" has been commodified, applied to everything from yoga apparel to luxury retreats. Yet behind these surface-level appropriations, the hunger for inner meaning remains. Individuals are still seeking a deeper truth that cannot be bought or branded. This is where Jung's original teachings regain their relevance: by inviting us to turn inward, not outward, to encounter the 'Self'.

Contemporary psychology, particularly in transpersonal and depth traditions, continues to draw upon Jung's idea of the Self as a central organizing force of the psyche. However, mainstream therapeutic practices often neglect the symbolic and mythological dimensions that make individuation so rich. CBT and behavioural models, while effective for symptom relief, rarely engage the deeper existential questions that the Self raises: Who am I beneath my roles? What is my soul asking of me?

In contrast, Jungian practitioners today use dream analysis, active imagination, and archetypal inquiry to help individuals listen to the voice of the Self. These practices offer an alternative to diagnosis and pathology by treating the psyche as a sacred terrain, not just a clinical problem.

Still, even within Jungian circles, the risk of romanticizing the Self persists. Some seekers mistake the Self for a final destination, an enlightenment badge to be worn with pride. But the Self, as Jung warned, is not something to be possessed or conquered. It is a living mystery. To encounter it is to stand in humility before the unknown.

In this way, the modern misinterpretations of the Self mirror the ego's attempt to control and codify what must remain fluid. But the true path of individuation remains clear: it is not a destination, but a continual unfolding. The Self does not shout, it whispers. And it is only when we silence the noise of performance that we can hear it speak.

Integration and the Future of the Self

The journey toward the Self does not conclude with understanding or symbolic visions, it culminates in integration. This is where the abstract becomes embodied. Integration involves bringing our insights down from the mountaintop and into the kitchen, the workplace, the argument, and the moment of fear. It is here where inner work meets outer life, and where transformation is tested by the texture of the everyday.

To integrate the Self means to live in a way that reflects wholeness rather than fragmentation. It means no longer denying, projecting, or dissociating from the parts of us that once seemed unacceptable. Instead, we live as one complex, authentic presence, imperfect but undivided.

Integration also has a collective dimension. As more individuals undergo this inner work, they influence the culture around them. Relationships deepen, communities become more conscious, and values shift from competition toward connection. In this way,

Jung's model was never just about personal healing. It was a vision for cultural renewal.

In the context of 21st-century complexity, climate crises, social upheaval, and rapid technological acceleration, the process of individuation offers a deeply human counterbalance. It anchors us in meaning. It reminds us that while we may not control the world, we can become responsible stewards of our inner terrain.

As we look to the future, the Self remains not a static answer, but an invitation. It invites us into deeper presence, greater responsibility, and a more expansive sense of belonging, not just to ourselves, but to the soul of the world.

The Rise of the Inner Revolution

The Modern Renaissance of Shadow Work

In recent years, shadow work has experienced a significant resurgence, propelled by the convergence of social media, therapy culture, and spiritual communities. This revival reflects a collective yearning for deeper self-understanding and healing.

Platforms like TikTok have played a pivotal role in popularizing shadow work. The viral success of resources such as *The Shadow Work Journal* by Keila Shaheen, which encourages users to confront repressed qualities, underscores this trend. While these tools offer accessible entry points into self-exploration, some critics argue they may oversimplify Carl Jung's complex theories, focusing narrowly on the shadow aspect and neglecting other components of the psyche *(teenvogue.com, theguardian.com)*.

Therapy culture has also embraced shadow work, integrating it into practices aimed at trauma healing and personal growth. Therapists incorporate shadow work into sessions to help clients process grief, intergenerational trauma, and other deep-seated issues. *(scienceofpeople.com, letsgethappi.com, teenvogue.com)*

Spiritual communities have recognized the importance of shadow work in fostering self-awareness and authenticity. Practices such as journaling, mindfulness meditation, and group engagement are employed to confront and integrate shadow aspects, leading to transformative personal and communal experiences *(transpersonal-psychology, iresearchnet.com)*.

This modern renaissance of shadow work signifies a shift towards embracing the complexities of the human psyche. By confronting and integrating our shadow aspects, individuals embark on a journey toward wholeness, authenticity, and deeper connection with themselves and their communities.

Trauma Awareness and the Healing Industry

In recent years, the integration of shadow work into trauma-informed therapeutic practices has gained significant traction. This evolution reflects a broader understanding of the interconnectedness between psychological trauma and the unconscious aspects of the self.

The Convergence of Shadow Work and Trauma Therapy

Shadow work, rooted in Carl Jung's concept of the "shadow", the unconscious parts of the psyche that individuals often repress, has found a place in modern trauma therapy. Therapists incorporate shadow work into sessions to help clients process grief, intergenerational trauma, and other deep-seated issues. By confronting these hidden aspects, individuals can achieve greater self-awareness and emotional healing. *(betterhelp.com)*

Somatic Approaches to Healing

The recognition that trauma is not only psychological but also physiological has led to the adoption of somatic therapies. Somatic Experiencing (SE), developed by Dr. Peter Levine, focuses on bodily sensations to release trauma stored in the nervous system. Similarly, Brain spotting, introduced by Dr. David Grand, uses eye positioning to access and process traumatic memories. These methods align with shadow work by addressing the unconscious manifestations of trauma in the body. *(self.com, en.wikipedia.org, workplacepeaceinstitute.com, en.wikipedia.org)*

The Commercialization of Healing

As the demand for trauma-informed practices grows, the wellness industry has responded with a plethora of products and services. Shadow work journals, online courses, and retreats promise rapid transformation. While these resources can be beneficial, there is a risk of oversimplifying complex psychological processes. Experts caution against the commodification of healing, emphasizing the importance of professional guidance.

Integrating Shadow Work into Daily Life

Beyond therapy sessions, individuals are encouraged to engage in shadow work through practices like journaling, meditation, and mindfulness. These activities foster a continuous process of self-reflection and integration, allowing for the gradual healing of trauma. By acknowledging and embracing the shadow, individuals can move toward a more authentic and balanced existence. *(counselling-directory.org.uk)*

From Depth to Trend: Risks of Oversimplification

In recent years, shadow work has surged in popularity, permeating social media platforms, self-help literature, and wellness communities. While this widespread interest reflects a collective yearning for self-understanding, it also brings the risk of oversimplifying Carl Jung's intricate theories.

One prominent example is the viral success of *The Shadow Work Journal* by Keila Shaheen, which has amassed over a billion views on TikTok. The journal encourages users to confront repressed qualities, often leading to emotional revelations. However, critics argue that it oversimplifies Jung's complex ideas, focusing narrowly on the shadow and neglecting other archetypes. While it offers a structured approach to introspection, it lacks depth and can be misleading without professional guidance. *(theguardian.com)*

This trend towards commodifying shadow work into easily digestible formats, such as workbooks, online courses, and social media challenges, risks reducing a profound psychological process into a checklist of tasks. Such approaches may neglect the nuanced understanding required to navigate the unconscious mind safely and effectively.

Furthermore, the commercialization of shadow work can lead to a superficial engagement with one's inner world. Without the guidance of trained professionals, individuals may misinterpret their experiences, leading to confusion or distress. As noted by experts, engaging with the shadow self can be unsettling, as it may feel like an external force is encroaching upon one's being. This sensation stems from illuminating and releasing repressed traumas and emotions, which can trigger the nervous system's fight or flight response. *(grace-being.com)*

Moreover, the oversimplification of shadow work may inadvertently reinforce harmful stereotypes or cultural biases. Jung's concept of the shadow encompasses not only personal unconscious elements but also collective unconscious aspects, which include societal norms and archetypes. Reducing this complexity to a singular focus on individual traits may overlook the broader cultural and systemic influences on the psyche. *(emotionalhealthcoaching.com)*

In conclusion, while the democratization of shadow work has made Jungian concepts more accessible, it is crucial to approach this inner work with depth, care, and professional support. Engaging with the shadow requires more than surface-level exercises; it demands a commitment to understanding the multifaceted nature of the unconscious and its influence on our lives.

Global Movements and the Democratization of Inner Work

In recent years, shadow work has transcended its roots in Jungian psychology to become a global phenomenon, embraced by diverse cultures and communities as a tool for personal and collective transformation. This democratization of inner work reflects a growing recognition of the interconnectedness between individual healing and societal change.

Shadow Work as a Catalyst for Social Justice

The global outcry following the murder of George Floyd in 2020 exemplifies how collective shadow work can catalyse social movements. Protests erupted worldwide, with demonstrators confronting systemic racism and historical injustices. In Australia, large-scale protests highlighted the deaths of Aboriginal people in police custody, prompting legislative responses and inquiries into systemic issues. These movements underscore the role of shadow work in acknowledging and addressing the "collective shadow", the societal and historical traumas that shape our communities. *(time.com)*

Integrating Shadow Work into Spiritual and Community Practices

Beyond activism, shadow work has been integrated into spiritual and community practices. Organizations like Coming to the Table facilitate dialogues between descendants of enslaved people and slave owners, fostering healing through the acknowledgment of historical traumas. Similarly, the Inner Work Community offers virtual opportunities for individuals to engage in shadow work within a spiritual formation context, bridging psychological and theological frameworks. *(digitalcommons.georgefox.edu)*

Challenges and Opportunities in the Global Expansion of Shadow Work

While the global embrace of shadow work offers opportunities for healing and growth, it also presents challenges. The commodification of shadow work through social media trends and commercial products risks oversimplifying complex psychological processes. Critics caution against the potential for misinterpretation and the dilution of Jung's original concepts. To maintain the integrity of shadow work, it is essential to approach these practices with depth, cultural sensitivity, and professional guidance. *(theguardian.com)*

In conclusion, the global movements embracing shadow work signify a collective yearning for authenticity, healing, and transformation. By confronting both personal and societal shadows, individuals and communities can foster a more conscious and compassionate world. *(gettherapybirmingham.com)*

The Return to Symbolic Literacy

In an age dominated by data and digital interfaces, a quiet yet profound shift is occurring: a resurgence of symbolic literacy. This movement reflects a collective yearning to reconnect with the rich, symbolic language of the unconscious, a language that offers depth, meaning, and a bridge between the conscious and unconscious realms.

Jung's Perspective on Symbols

Carl Jung emphasized the importance of symbols as vital expressions of the unconscious mind. In his seminal work, *Man and His Symbols*, Jung described symbols as the best possible expression for something unknown, highlighting their role in conveying aspects of the psyche that are not easily articulated through rational thought. He believed that engaging with symbols, arising from dreams, myths, and cultural narratives, was essential for achieving psychological wholeness and self-understanding. *(en.wikipedia.org, mentalzon.com)*

Dreams as a Gateway to the Unconscious

Dreams serve as a primary avenue through which symbols emerge, offering insights into both personal and collective unconscious processes. Jung viewed dreams as communications from the unconscious, utilizing symbolic imagery to reveal repressed emotions, unresolved conflicts, and potential paths toward individuation. By analysing dream symbols, individuals can uncover hidden aspects of themselves and facilitate personal growth. *(books.google.com)*

The Role of Myth and Culture

Mythology and cultural narratives are rich sources of symbolic content, reflecting universal themes and archetypes that resonate across time and societies. Jung asserted that myths are manifestations of the collective unconscious, providing frameworks through which individuals can understand their experiences and navigate life's challenges. Engaging with myths allows for a deeper connection to shared human experiences and the archetypal patterns that shape our psyches. *(dreamsmean.org)*

Personal Interpretation and Active Imagination

Jung advocated for the personal interpretation of symbols, emphasizing that their meanings are not fixed but vary based on individual experiences and contexts. He introduced the technique of active imagination, encouraging individuals to engage with symbols through creative expression, such as art, writing, or visualization. This process fosters a dialogue between the conscious and unconscious, facilitating the integration of disparate aspects of the self. *(mythsdreamssymbols.com)*

Modern Applications and the Revival of Symbolic Understanding

In contemporary times, there is a renewed interest in symbolic literacy, evident in the popularity of practices like dream analysis, tarot, astrology, and mythological studies. These modalities offer individuals tools to explore their inner worlds, understand their unconscious motivations, and find meaning in their experiences. The resurgence of symbolic engagement reflects a collective desire to move beyond surface-level understanding and reconnect with the deeper layers of the psyche.

The return to symbolic literacy signifies a vital shift in our collective consciousness, emphasizing the importance of engaging with the rich, symbolic language of the unconscious. By embracing symbols, dreams, and myths, individuals can embark on a transformative journey toward self-discovery, healing, and psychological integration. This renewed focus on symbolic understanding offers a pathway to deeper meaning and wholeness in an increasingly complex and fragmented world.

Critiques from Academia and Traditional Psychology

As shadow work gains popularity in contemporary culture, it has attracted critical attention from academic and traditional psychological perspectives. Scholars and practitioners have raised concerns about the oversimplification, cultural biases, and potential misapplications of Jungian concepts in modern contexts.

Oversimplification and Commodification

The viral success of resources like *The Shadow Work Journal* by Keila Shaheen illustrates the mainstream appeal of shadow work. However, critics argue that such tools often reduce complex Jungian theories to simplistic exercises, neglecting the depth and nuance inherent in the original concepts. This commodification risks trivializing the transformative potential of shadow work, turning it into a marketable trend rather than a profound psychological process.

Cultural and Colonial Biases

Jung's theories have been critiqued for their Eurocentric and colonial underpinnings. His emphasis on universal archetypes and the collective unconscious has been seen as a means of abstracting and decontextualizing cultural narratives, potentially marginalizing non-Western perspectives. This critique calls for a more culturally sensitive approach to shadow work that acknowledges and respects diverse cultural contexts.

Potential for Misuse in Relationships

In interpersonal contexts, shadow work can be misapplied, leading to issues such as over-psychologizing or spiritual bypassing. For instance, individuals might attribute relational conflicts solely to their partner's unresolved shadow aspects, thereby avoiding accountability and dismissing legitimate concerns. Such misuses underscore the importance of ethical considerations and the need for professional guidance when engaging in shadow work within relationships. *(danieldashnawcouplestherapy.com)*

Integration with Traditional Therapeutic Practices

While shadow work offers valuable insights, traditional psychology emphasizes evidence-based practices and empirical validation. Some practitioners caution against relying solely on shadow work for psychological healing, advocating for its integration with established therapeutic modalities to ensure comprehensive care. This perspective encourages a balanced approach that combines the introspective depth of shadow work with the structured methodologies of conventional therapy.

In summary, while shadow work has the potential to facilitate profound personal growth, it is essential to approach it with critical awareness. Recognizing its limitations, cultural implications, and the necessity for professional support can help individuals engage with shadow work more responsibly and effectively.

Living the Work: Integration in Daily Life

Shadow work is not merely a theoretical concept, or a set of exercises confined to therapy sessions; it is a continuous, lived experience that permeates every aspect of daily life. The integration of the shadow, the unconscious parts of ourselves that we often deny or suppress, is essential for achieving psychological wholeness and authenticity. This process involves acknowledging and embracing these hidden aspects, leading to profound personal growth and transformation. *(zensound.co.uk)*

Daily Practices for Shadow Integration

Incorporating shadow work into everyday life requires intentional practices that foster self-awareness and acceptance. Journaling is a powerful tool for this purpose. By writing about emotional reactions, especially those that are intense or negative, individuals can uncover underlying patterns and triggers. For instance, noting instances of irritation or jealousy can reveal repressed traits or unmet needs. *(thecollector.com)*

Dream analysis is another avenue for engaging with the shadow. Dreams often serve as messages from the unconscious, presenting symbols and narratives that reflect our inner conflicts and desires. Keeping a dream journal and reflecting on recurring themes can provide insights into aspects of the self that require attention and integration. *(zensound.co.uk, thecollector.com)*

Creative expression, such as drawing, painting, or storytelling, allows the unconscious to surface in a non-verbal form. These activities can bypass the rational mind, enabling individuals to explore and integrate shadow aspects through symbolism and metaphor.

Impact on Relationships

Integrating the shadow has significant implications for interpersonal relationships. By becoming aware of our projections, attributes we unconsciously assign to others, we can reduce misunderstandings and conflicts. This awareness fosters empathy and authentic connections, as we recognize and accept both our own and others' complexities. *(theelementalmind.com, cpja.org.uk, thestandupphilosophers.co.uk)*

Embracing the Ongoing Journey

Shadow work is not a one-time endeavour but a lifelong journey of self-discovery and growth. It requires ongoing commitment to self-reflection, acceptance, and the courage to confront uncomfortable truths. By consistently engaging with our shadow, we cultivate a more integrated and authentic self, capable of navigating life's challenges with resilience and compassion.

Soul, Symbol, and the Sacred Psyche

Spiritual Dimensions of Shadow Work

While Carl Jung firmly grounded his work in psychological observation, he never shied away from the sacred. He believed that spiritual experience was not outside the psyche but rather a central component of it. In fact, one of the most radical aspects of Jungian theory is the idea that the search for meaning, for God, for wholeness, for the divine, is inextricably linked to the psyche's natural longing for integration. In this view, shadow work is not just emotional or psychological healing. It is also a spiritual path.

Jung was careful not to promote any one religious framework. Instead, he studied myths, alchemy, Eastern philosophies, and Christian mysticism to understand the symbolic language of the soul. He saw that the human psyche speaks in symbols, and these symbols often mirror religious or mythological motifs. Dreams of light and dark, serpents and angels, caves and mountaintops, these are not merely figments of imagination, but indicators of inner transformation.

When individuals engage in shadow work, they begin to unearth parts of themselves long denied or feared. This confrontation often takes on a spiritual quality. People report feeling as though they are in a dark night of the soul, or that they are experiencing a kind of psychic death and rebirth. Jung saw this not as pathology, but as part of the individuation process, a sacred initiation into deeper selfhood.

The Language of Symbols

Symbolism lies at the heart of Jung's psychological approach. He believed that symbols are the bridge between the conscious and unconscious mind. They arise from the archetypal layer of the psyche, which holds universal images and patterns that transcend personal experience. A snake in a dream might signal transformation. A house with many rooms could suggest unexplored parts of the self. A sudden flood could symbolize emotional overwhelm or cleansing.

These symbols are not fixed in meaning. They must be interpreted within the personal context of the dreamer or seeker. This makes shadow work a profoundly individual journey, where the psyche itself becomes the oracle. Active imagination, dream journaling, art, and creative ritual all serve as methods for engaging this symbolic dialogue.

Jung did not believe the unconscious was simply a repository of discarded material. He saw it as intelligent, purposive, and inherently sacred. The unconscious is not just where we bury pain, it is where the soul speaks. And if we are willing to listen, we may hear the voice of the Self whispering through our darkest places.

Modern Practices and Sacred Psychology

In the 21st century, the spiritual dimension of shadow work has been embraced in various fields, including transpersonal psychology, integrative therapy, and even secular mindfulness traditions. While mainstream psychology still favours evidence-based modalities, many clinicians and coaches are drawing from

Jung's legacy to create hybrid methods that honor both the psychological and the spiritual.

Practices such as somatic experiencing, inner child work, and psychedelic-assisted therapy often echo Jungian principles, even if not explicitly labelled as such. These methods recognize that healing requires more than cognitive insight. It requires embodied transformation, an encounter with the sacred, however one defines it.

Communities and individuals across the globe are turning to these integrative practices to address trauma, depression, anxiety, and existential emptiness. The language of "parts work," "soul retrieval," and "inner alchemy" is becoming more common, not only in therapy but in social media, wellness spaces, and spiritual communities. Jung's concept of the Self as a sacred centre resonates deeply in a world that increasingly feels fragmented and disenchanted.

Toward a Sacred Reconnection

The final movement of shadow work is not simply self-knowledge. It is reconnection, to one's inner life, to others, to the world, and perhaps to the divine. As individuals come to terms with their shadow, they often find a deeper sense of purpose emerging. Compassion grows. Integrity strengthens. Life no longer feels random but infused with symbolic meaning.

This is not dogma. It is direct experience. It is the moment someone realizes that their pain was never punishment but invitation. That the inner monsters were misunderstood messengers. That their wounds, once honored, become wombs of creation.

Jung never offered a final answer to the question of God. But he did believe that each person carries within them a sacred image, a potential for wholeness that longs to be realized. Shadow work is the portal. The psyche is the path. And the Self is the silent, shining flame that guides the way.

This chapter closes the circle not with conclusion, but with invitation. The reader is urged not to worship Jung, nor Freud, nor any method. But to follow the deepest whisper of their own soul, wherever it may lead.

The Collective Shadow and Cultural Healing

In every culture, in every era, the shadow does not remain confined to the individual. It spills outward, shaping society, systems, ideologies, and institutions. Jung understood that what we repress personally, we often project collectively. Injustices, scapegoating, systemic oppression, and even war can all be seen as manifestations of the unintegrated collective shadow. What one refuses to face inwardly is eventually acted out outwardly.

Jung wrote in *The Undiscovered Self* that "the gigantic catastrophes that threaten us today are not elemental happenings of a physical or biological order, but psychic events." For him, the external chaos of the 20th century, and by extension, the 21st, was rooted in psychological fragmentation. When we split off aspects of ourselves, denying the fear, envy, rage, or grief we carry, those same forces begin to move through the collective body of society. Prejudice, polarization, and violence are not merely political or economic problems; they are psychological symptoms.

This understanding opens a radical lens for cultural transformation. Healing the world requires more than policy changes or protests. It requires inner work. Each time an individual confronts their shadow, they contribute to the collective integration of human consciousness. Each time someone breaks a cycle of projection, blames less, listens more, and takes responsibility for their inner world, they participate in cultural healing.

This is not to suggest that systemic issues are reducible to inner psychology, oppression must be dismantled on the outside as well. But without attending to the unconscious forces that drive these patterns, we risk repeating history in new forms. The collective shadow morphs: from colonialism to corporate exploitation, from dogma to digital manipulation, from war to ideological warfare. The outer forms shift, but the underlying disownment of shadow remains.

Jung's writings anticipated much of what we are now witnessing in global culture. He warned of mass-mindedness, the rise of archetypal possession, and the dangers of unexamined group identity. He urged individuals to cultivate awareness, lest they be swept up by collective currents they do not understand. The loss of the individual soul, he believed, was the greatest threat to civilization.

In this context, shadow work becomes more than personal growth. It becomes a kind of ethical and spiritual activism. To do the inner work is to disrupt the unconscious inheritance of hatred and fear. To reflect before reacting, to examine one's own complicity, to humanize the "other", these are not passive acts. They are soul revolutions. They are how we interrupt the unconscious programming of history.

The path of the inner activist is quiet. It doesn't parade its virtue. But it creates ripples. A parent becomes less reactive, and a child grows up with more emotional safety. A leader becomes more self-aware, and a community becomes more resilient. An artist reclaims their pain and turns it into beauty, inspiring healing in those who witness it. This is the work of cultural alchemy: not to escape the world, but to redeem it from within.

Jung believed that integration must begin with the individual. But he also knew that true individuation cannot occur in isolation. The Self does not emerge in a vacuum. It is shaped, tested, and refined in relationship, to others, to nature, to the world. The more whole a person becomes, the more capable they are of compassion, nuance, and vision. And the more visionary individuals we have, the more likely we are to build cultures of soul.

We live in a time of great unravelling, ecological, social, political. But this unravelling also reveals what has been hidden. It exposes what no longer serves. In this moment of reckoning, we are invited to meet not just our personal shadows, but the shadow of our species. We are called to look at history not to shame, but to understand. To gaze into the mirror of time not to condemn, but to choose differently.

Cultural healing is slow. It requires patience and humility. But it begins with each act of inner clarity, each refusal to other, each step toward wholeness. As Jung wrote, "Who looks outside dreams, who looks inside awakens." The world is waiting for us to awaken. Not into perfection, but into presence. Not into dogma, but into dialogue. Not into ideology, but into integration.

The collective shadow will not be solved by force. It will be softened by truth. It will be transformed not by dominance, but by depth. And that depth begins wherever we are willing to be honest, with ourselves, with each other, and with the inheritance we carry.

Integration in Practice

Nine Tools, Techniques, and Daily Rituals

1. From Insight to Action

There comes a moment in the inner journey when reflection is no longer enough. Insights accumulate like puzzle pieces on a table, but unless assembled into action, they remain scattered. This is the turning point, from understanding our shadow to integrating it. True transformation demands embodiment. It's not what we know intellectually, but how we live it moment by moment that rewires the psyche.

Shadow work, then, becomes less about isolated breakthroughs and more about building emotional stamina. Integration is not flashy. It's quiet and persistent. It's in how we speak to our partners when we feel unseen. It's in the pause before lashing out, the breath before repeating a familiar pattern, the willingness to sit with discomfort without needing to numb it.

While the earlier chapters explored the roots and theory of shadow psychology, what follows is a return to the ordinary, sacred daily ground, the place where real change happens.

We begin with the body.

---

2. Returning to the Body

If the shadow lives in the unconscious, its echo is carried in the body. Long before the mind can name a wound, the body knows. It clenches, withdraws, flares, numbs. Somatic memory holds the pain we couldn't process, the truths we weren't safe to speak. This is why integration begins below awareness, beneath cognition, inside sensation.

Jung hinted at this through his deep respect for the body's symbolic expressions. Though less systematized than modern somatic practices, his work opened the door to what we now recognize: that trauma is not just psychological, it is physiological. Shadow material is stored in the nervous system. To integrate it, we must learn to feel again, safely, slowly, and without judgment.

Daily shadow work asks for a return to the body as teacher. Practices like mindful breathwork, body scanning, or gentle movement (such as yoga or intuitive stretching) help reestablish internal connection. These acts signal to the nervous system that it's safe to explore. When we are regulated, we can feel without overwhelm. We can witness without collapsing.

Some find embodiment through nature, bare feet in the grass, ocean salt on skin, wind against the face. These are not escapes from shadow, but doorways into it. They remind us that the body is not the enemy. It is the container. The shadow doesn't need to be purged, it longs to be held.

Embodiment also invites the integration of pleasure. Often, shadow work is imagined as heavy, serious, painful. But joy, too, is a part of wholeness. Many people exile their joy just as deeply as their anger. To feel pleasure without guilt, to receive touch without shame, to laugh without defensiveness, these are also forms of integration.

Coming back to the body is not a one-time awakening. It is a practice of reinhabiting the present. In the body, time slows. Clarity sharpens. The stories we carry begin to unravel, not through force, but through somatic honesty. And in this honesty, shadow becomes sensation, sensation becomes insight, and insight becomes freedom.

3. Dialogue with the Unconscious

The unconscious speaks in symbols, images, moods, and metaphor. It does not speak the language of logic, but the language of dreams, poetry, and gut instinct. To engage the shadow is to open a dialogue, not a confrontation, but a conversation. And like all conversations worth having, it begins with listening.

Carl Jung developed a method called *active imagination*, a way to interact with the contents of the unconscious without analysis or suppression. It involves allowing an image, mood, or dream fragment to surface, and then entering into imaginative interaction with it, through writing, drawing, or inner dialogue. You might speak to the angry child inside you. You might ask a shadowy figure in a dream why it keeps returning. You might allow a symbol, a key, a cave, a mirror, to reveal its meaning. These are not games. They are rituals of re-integration.

Journaling is one of the most accessible ways to practice this dialogue. But shadow journaling differs from surface-level diary entries. It asks, "What am I afraid to admit?" It asks, "What emotion was I trying to avoid today?" It dares to track recurring patterns, jealousy in friendships, shame in sexuality, rage at authority. Writing brings the unconscious into the visible. And what is made visible can be made whole.

Dreamwork also plays a central role. Jung called dreams the "royal road" to the unconscious. Keeping a dream journal and reflecting on symbols over time can reveal hidden drives, unresolved wounds, or intuitive guidance. Rather than decoding dreams like puzzles, Jung encouraged seeing each element of the dream as part of the Self. The shadow may appear as a pursuer, a trickster, a seductive stranger. To face them is to greet the fragmented parts of our own psyche.

Art can be another portal. When words fail, drawing, painting, or sculpting the inner landscape can give form to the formless. The unconscious loves symbol. Let your hand move without judgment. What emerges may not be pretty, but it will be true.

These dialogues are not about answers. They are about contact. The goal is not to conquer the shadow, but to enter into a sacred relationship with it. In doing so, we reclaim what has been lost. We speak with the silence inside us. And we begin to trust that the unconscious is not our enemy, but our mirror.

4. Creating Sacred Containers

Shadow work is deep, often destabilizing. Without structure, the psyche can feel as if it's unravelling rather than integrating. This is why sacred containers matter. They don't constrain the work, they hold it. They create the safety necessary for descent, the ritual space where the unseen can be made visible, and the painful can become purposeful.

A sacred container doesn't have to be religious or elaborate. It can be as simple as lighting a candle before journaling, dedicating a quiet corner of the room for inner work, or marking time with ritual language, "I am entering," "I am returning." The act of naming the space invites the unconscious to speak and the conscious self to listen. Ritual builds trust.

Symbolic acts are especially powerful in shadow integration. Writing a letter you'll never send. Burying a representation of a former identity. Burning the shame story you've carried since childhood. These are gestures of intention. They speak to the unconscious in its own tongue, not through explanation, but through embodiment.

Altars or visual symbols can serve as focal points. You might place a feather to represent freedom from projection, a stone for grounded truth, an object from childhood to welcome the wounded inner child home. These symbols evolve with the journey. Over time, they form a living mirror of the soul's process.

The cycles of nature offer another sacred rhythm. Solstices and equinoxes, full moons and new moons, changing seasons, all offer archetypal resonance for inner work. The inner world responds to outer movement. When you align shadow rituals with these natural cycles, you tether the psyche to something larger. You remember you are part of a greater unfolding.

Some draw upon ancestral practices or indigenous wisdom for ritual structure. When done with respect and self-awareness, not appropriation, these lineages can offer profound support. It's important to listen to the origin of these traditions and engage them in ways that honor their roots.

The point is not to make shadow work mystical for its own sake, but to make it meaningful. Sacred containers make space for grief, rage, confusion, release. They remind us that we are not broken, we are becoming. And when held with reverence, even the darkest truths can find a place in the circle of light.

5. Rewriting the Inner Narrative

Every person walks through life with a story, often invisible, often inherited. It begins in childhood and gets reinforced by relationships, environments, culture, and trauma. "I'm too much." "I'm not enough." "If I fail, I'll be abandoned." These narratives are not just thoughts. They're survival blueprints. And most of them are written by the shadow.

Shadow work reveals these scripts not to erase them, but to rewrite them. To revise the roles we've been cast into without consent. This is not about affirmation without depth; it's about authorship. To take back the pen and say, "This is who I was told I was. Now let me find out who I truly am."

Language is a powerful tool of integration. The words we speak inside our minds shape the identities we inhabit. When you start to hear your inner critic say, "I always sabotage things," and you respond with, "I'm learning to pause and choose differently," you are not lying, you are rewriting. It's not delusion. It's re-narration. And it matters.

But rewriting doesn't always come in neat sentences. Sometimes it arrives in symbols. Archetypal embodiment, living as the sovereign, the healer, the truth-teller, can help us shift identity from wounded to whole. Jung understood that we live through psychic patterns far older than we are. By naming them, invoking them, and stepping into their wisdom, we expand our sense of self.

That's why storytelling is so essential in healing. Whether through journaling, therapy, poetry, or simple conversation, telling your story from a new perspective makes space for evolution. "This happened to me" becomes "This shaped me." "I failed" becomes "I adapted." "I was betrayed" becomes "I learned the limits of trust, and how to rebuild it."

Some may resist this as self-deception. But rewriting isn't pretending things didn't happen. It's choosing how they live in your system now. Are they anchors or teachers? Curses or initiations?

To reclaim the narrative is to no longer be ruled by the unspoken. It is to recognize that the story you carry is not fixed. It's alive. And like all living things, it can grow, if you let it.

6. The Role of Relationship in Integration

No matter how deep our inner work goes, we cannot fully meet the shadow without others. Relationship is where our wounds are exposed, our defence's tested, and our hidden parts mirrored back to us. If solitude is where awareness begins, intimacy is where integration is forged.

Jung understood that the psyche is not a sealed-off chamber. It is porous. It meets the world constantly, especially through other people. The shadow is rarely more visible than in the way we react to those closest to us. The partner who triggers our need for control. The friend who makes us feel invisible. The colleague who stirs envy. These are not random annoyances. They are doorways into disowned parts of ourselves.

Relational triggers are invitations. When anger surges or withdrawal tempts, we can ask, "What part of me is being touched here?" Often, it is a younger self, a forgotten hurt, or a truth we have denied. The challenge is not to avoid these moments but to stay with them long enough to understand.

Projection is one of the core mechanisms of the shadow in relationship. We assign our unwanted traits to others, so we don't have to face them in ourselves. We see arrogance, when really, we fear our own voice. We see weakness, when really, we despise our own vulnerability. When we reclaim these projections, we reduce conflict and increase intimacy, not because we become perfect, but because we become honest.

Conscious communication becomes a tool of integration. Instead of blame, we use "I" statements. Instead of reacting, we pause and reflect. Instead of assuming, we ask. This doesn't mean becoming passive. Integration requires boundaries, clarity, and truth. But it also requires curiosity. Why does this person's behaviour bother me so deeply? What part of me have I forgotten in this dynamic?

Romantic relationships, especially, can activate the deepest shadows. They echo early attachments. They surface abandonment fears, control needs, and unmet longing. But they also offer a space to heal, if both partners are willing to do the work. Sometimes the most profound integration happens not when we find someone to complete us, but when we see how we project completion onto others.

Friendships, too, become sacred mirrors. In community, we encounter parts of ourselves we never knew were waiting for contact. In conflict, we see our edges. In love, we see what we forgot we deserved.

Integration in relationship is not about harmony at all costs. It is about depth. It's about staying present through rupture and repair. It's about becoming brave enough to say, "This is who I am," and soft enough to hear the same from another.

7. Resistance, Fatigue, and Spiritual Bypassing

Shadow work, like all true transformation, is not linear. There are moments of clarity followed by confusion, moments of courage followed by collapse. This is not failure. It is rhythm. Resistance is not a sign that you are doing something wrong, it is a sign that you are approaching something real.

The psyche resists integration not out of malice, but out of habit. It has survived by keeping certain truths hidden. Defence mechanisms are, at their core, acts of protection. When we begin to dissolve them, the system trembles. The familiar, even if painful, feels safer than the unknown. This is why many people experience fatigue during inner work. Emotional labour drains the body. Cognitive reframing exhausts the mind. It is natural to feel the weight of it.

But fatigue is not a signal to give up. It is a signal to pace. Integration requires rest. There are times to explore and times to restore. There is wisdom in stepping back, letting the soil settle after it's been stirred. Some days, the most shadow-aware act is to drink water, take a walk, and feel the sun on your face without needing to uncover anything deeper.

Alongside resistance, there is another trap: spiritual bypassing. This is when we use high-minded ideas to avoid emotional reality. It often sounds like: "Everything happens for a reason," or "It's all love and light." These phrases, while well-intentioned, can obscure pain rather than illuminate it. They are masks worn by fear. They bypass the rawness of grief, the depth of anger, the honesty of sorrow.

True spirituality doesn't bypass the shadow. It includes it. It kneels beside the pain and says, "You are part of me too." Jung warned of this tendency to idealize the light while repressing the dark. He wrote, "One does not become enlightened by imagining figures of light, but by making the darkness conscious."

Integration asks us to hold both, the part that longs for transcendence, and the part that aches for validation. It asks us to see where we use intellect, productivity, or positivity to sidestep the deeper layers. And when we catch ourselves doing it, we don't need to judge. We just begin again, a little more gently this time.

Resistance is part of the path. So is fatigue. So is forgetting. The gift of shadow work is that it welcomes all of it. You don't need to push through. You need only return. And in the returning, wholeness finds you again.

8. The Soul's Daily Practice

Integration is not a destination. It is a devotion. A daily rhythm. A subtle agreement we make with ourselves, not to be perfect, but to be present. Not to conquer the shadow once and for all, but to keep company with it, to understand it, to grow alongside it.

The soul does not demand grand gestures. It responds to consistency. Morning silence before the world speaks. A journal waiting on the bedside. A breath before a reply. A single question whispered into the night: "What did I avoid today?" These are not small things. They are sacred repetitions, the soul's quiet rituals of return.

Daily shadow practice can be as brief as five minutes. The power lies in the intention, not the length. Choose a time of day where your mind is soft and your heart is open. It could be morning, before tasks take over. It could be evening, as you digest what the day revealed. Create a simple ritual to begin, lighting a candle, breathing deeply, opening a favorite quote or archetypal image.

Then ask yourself what part of you went unseen today. Was there a moment of jealousy you buried? A desire you dismissed? A truth you swallowed? Name it. Greet it. Let it speak. You are not there to fix it, only to feel it. You may choose to journal or simply sit with what arises. Let the shadow be a guest, not a threat.

You can also make space for daily affirmations, not in the sense of surface positivity, but in the spirit of truth-telling. "I am willing to meet what I hide." "I am safe enough to feel." "I do not need to shame myself to grow." These are not wishes. They are vows.

Movement can be integrated too. A short walk with no destination. A song that lets you move your hips, your grief, your history. Some days, the body speaks when words cannot. Let it.

Over time, these small rituals weave a net beneath you. When life fractures you open, as it inevitably does, you will land inside a practice already in motion. The daily soul rhythm becomes your compass. It reminds you who you are beneath the story. It becomes your tether to self when the world feels too much.

And it will feel like too much sometimes. But the shadow is not asking you to handle it all at once. It's asking you to come closer. One breath at a time. One truth at a time. One sacred pause at a time.

9. Wholeness as a Way of Being

Integration is not a reward. It is not a final state of bliss we arrive at after enough work has been done. It is a way of being, ongoing, dynamic, imperfect. Wholeness means we no longer exile any part of ourselves, even the parts we once feared, rejected, or despised. We begin to live from the centre, not the edge.

Jung did not promise that individuation would make us happy. He warned, in fact, that it might be painful. But he believed it would make us real. And from that realness, raw and refined at once, comes freedom. The freedom to respond instead of reacting. The freedom to love without losing oneself. The freedom to suffer without shame, to rejoice without guilt, to live without fragmentation.

In a culture obsessed with improvement, shadow work teaches us something radical: we are not projects to fix, but mysteries to witness. The shadow is not our enemy. It is our missing history, our misnamed strength, our misunderstood hunger. When we make space for it, not to indulge it, but to understand it, we become more than our wounds. We become whole.

To live a life of integration is to become trustworthy to oneself. Not because we never falter, but because we know how to return. Again, and again. To truth. To tenderness. To the tangled beauty of being fully human.

This is the quiet revolution. The one that begins inside and radiates outward. It does not ask us to shine without flaw, but to illuminate the dark with presence. It does not ask us to escape the shadow, but to befriend it.

And in doing so, we become something rare in this world: whole, aware, and at peace, not because the shadow is gone, but because it is known.

As Jung wrote:
"I'd rather be whole than good."

Let that be our closing vow for this chapter: not to perform goodness, but to embody wholeness.

Echoes of Repression

How the Past Repeats

1. The Loop of the Unconscious

There are moments when life seems to echo itself, when the same kinds of people hurt us, the same fears return in different disguises, and the same disappointments wear new names. These repetitions are rarely coincidental. Freud called it *repetition compulsion*, a psychic loop in which the mind re-creates unresolved situations in the unconscious hope of mastering them. We return to the scene of the wound, repeatedly, not to suffer, but to resolve. Only we don't know that's what we're doing.

This cycle is not limited to trauma survivors or those with diagnosed conditions. It lives in nearly everyone. The partner who keeps falling for emotionally unavailable people. The leader who sabotages success at the peak of visibility. The friend who always finds themselves abandoned when they finally open up. These aren't just poor choices, they are unconscious patterns. And they speak the language of the shadow.

Freud observed this in his early case studies: a woman who attracted violent lovers, a man who sabotaged every job once praised, a patient who returned to illness after recovery. The psyche, he believed, is driven not only by pleasure, but by the compulsion to repeat what is unresolved. Jung expanded on this by exploring *why* we repeat. For him, it wasn't only about reenactment, it was about symbolic reintegration. The soul is not content with suppression. It longs for wholeness, even if it leads us into pain to get there.

These patterns are not punishment. They are the psyche's language of urgency. When something repeats, it wants our attention. It wants us to stop, listen, and look underneath. What unspoken belief drives this? What buried grief is asking to be known? What part of ourselves have we abandoned so completely that we can only meet it through projection?

In the modern world, we often mistake these loops for failure. "I thought I was over this." "I should have healed by now." But the truth is more compassionate: healing is not linear. It spirals. What comes back is not a sign of weakness, it's a sign of readiness. The pattern has returned not to torment you, but because you are finally strong enough to meet it differently.

And that is the moment when everything can begin to change. Not when the pattern stops, but when your response does. When you pause instead of reacting. When you ask instead of assuming. When you witness your own pain instead of blaming someone else for it. This is where shadow work meets liberation.

To recognize the loop is to begin to break it, not with force, but with awareness.

2. History Doesn't Repeat - It Rhymes

When the same story returns again and again, not only in personal life but across families, cultures, and centuries, we are not simply reliving the past. We are rhyming with it. These recurring patterns may shift form, but their emotional core remains the same. Betrayal, abandonment, power, shame, control, silence. The names change. The faces change. But the underlying pattern repeats until someone stops the rhythm and listens.

Jung saw this not only in the psyche of individuals but in the collective psyche of entire civilizations. He observed that societies repress what they cannot integrate and then unconsciously act it out through war, scapegoating, and ideological possession. What the individual denies within becomes, on a larger scale, cultural fate.

It is not that history *literally* repeats itself, but that we are so often unconscious of its emotional residue that we recreate it. In families, this shows up in the unresolved grief of grandparents that spills into the depression of grandchildren. In romantic relationships, it appears when a person unconsciously seeks out partners who will mirror the very rejection or neglect, they first experienced in childhood. Even in careers, people find themselves enacting the same self-sabotaging dynamics they saw modelled by parents or early role models, working to the point of collapse or shrinking from visibility, all the while unaware of the origin.

These are not just bad habits. They are unintegrated memories living in the body, in the nervous system, in the inherited stories we never question.

And they do not vanish on their own. They must be remembered, not to dwell in them, but to differentiate from them. Remembering gives us choice. It allows us to say, "This belongs to me," or "This does not." It allows us to act from consciousness, not compulsion.

Jung believed that the more unconscious material a person carries, the more likely they are to project it outward. And what is not transformed *is* transmitted, into the next generation, into a new relationship, into the next decision that echoes the wound instead of healing it.

This is not a call for blame. It is a call for courage. Because once we see the rhyme, we can change the verse.

> *"Until you make the unconscious conscious, it will direct your life and you will call it fate."*
> ~ Carl Gustav Jung

3. Childhood Scripts and Adult Roles

Our earliest emotional environment becomes the soil in which all future relationships are planted. Long before we speak, we absorb. We learn love through tone, safety through touch, shame through silence. These unspoken lessons shape how we connect, protect, and disconnect. And often, we are not living our adult lives, we are reliving our childhood scripts.

Jung saw these early patterns not merely as psychological conditioning, but as archetypal templates. The child internalizes not just a personal story but a universal drama: the abandoned one, the rejected one, the invisible one, the burdened one. These identities, often forged through early attachment wounds, become the lens through which the adult sees the world. Without integration, these stories continue playing on loop, not because they are true, but because they are familiar.

For Jung, the path forward required conscious individuation: becoming aware of the inherited roles and gently disidentifying from them. To become whole was to see clearly what one was never meant to carry.

Freud, by contrast, framed these developmental blueprints in strictly biological and psychosexual terms. His Oedipus complex theory suggested that a child's emotional life was primarily rooted in sexual tension and rivalry. He believed that boys unconsciously desired their mothers and feared their fathers, while girls experienced a form of penis envy and redirected desire toward their fathers. For Freud, these dynamics, whether they aligned with actual experience, were the foundation of adult neuroses. The cure, in his view, was found through uncovering these repressed drives and resolving them through analysis.

In this way, Freud saw adult dysfunction as rooted in improperly sublimated sexual instinct, while Jung viewed it more broadly as a loss of symbolic connection and soul integration. Where Freud saw pathology, Jung saw meaning. Where Freud reduced suffering to libido, Jung expanded it into myth.

This divergence is striking in their own words.

> *"The conscious mind may be compared to a fountain playing in the sun and falling back into the great subterranean pool of subconscious from which it rises."*
> ~ Sigmund Freud

> *"I am not what happened to me, I am what I choose to become."*
> ~ Carl Jung

Freud believed that much of our psychic life is governed by instinctual repression and unconscious desires shaped by family roles. Jung believed that those early experiences shaped the ego, but not the whole Self. He saw the potential for transformation beyond the family drama.

So, when we look at how childhood shapes adult roles, we must ask: Are we bound by drives, or called toward destiny? Are we products of forbidden desire, or participants in a soul story seeking wholeness? Perhaps the truth, as always, is in the tension between them.

4. Generational Echoes and Epigenetic Imprints

Not everything we carry is ours. Some burdens arrive silently, passed down not through stories, but through silence. The unwept tears of our grandmothers. The rage our fathers swallowed. The secrets that shaped the way our parents looked at us without ever speaking. Inherited trauma is not folklore, it is biology, psychology, and soul history, braided together in the human nervous system.

Freud touched this territory unknowingly. Though his focus was on the individual's psychosexual development, he frequently returned to the idea that repression begins in childhood, and that this repression often stems from the pressures and expectations of the prior generation. He saw the family unit as a microcosm of human neurosis, a stage where inherited rules and taboos were enforced, rebelled against, and internalized.

But Jung carried the idea further. To him, we are not just living out our personal history, we are also living the unlived lives of those who came before. "Nothing influences a child so much as the unlived life of the parent," he wrote. What was unspoken becomes implicit. What was unresolved becomes fate.

And now, science is catching up with what these thinkers intuited. The field of epigenetics has shown that trauma can leave chemical markers on DNA, changes that don't alter the genetic code itself but affect how genes are expressed. These markers can be passed down, making descendants more susceptible to stress, anxiety, or hypervigilance without any "logical" cause. Children of Holocaust survivors, Indigenous populations, descendants of enslaved people, all show evidence of inherited psychological and physiological responses rooted in collective trauma.

This is the shadow at scale: not just the unconscious of one person, but of an entire bloodline, carried forward unconsciously. A generation raised by survivors becomes fearful of joy. A child raised by emotionally distant parents learns not to expect intimacy. A young adult repeats the same abandonment, over and over, unaware that they're reenacting a grief that was never theirs to begin with.

To do shadow work in this context is not simply to heal yourself, it is to become the one who interrupts the inheritance. The one who names what was denied. The one who chooses not to pass it on. And this doesn't mean rejecting our lineage. It means honoring it by telling the truth about it.

Jung believed that the integration of these inherited patterns was essential to the individuation process. He called it the "ancestral shadow", those collective energies that must be made conscious for true freedom to be possible. Freud, too, recognized the influence of parental authority and moral inheritance but confined it to the Oedipal drama. Jung expanded it to myth, symbol, and archetype, realms in which ancestral pain could be transformed, not merely analysed.

We now know what is not addressed becomes embodied. What is not expressed becomes depression. What is not healed is handed down.

But the good news is this: the moment we become aware, the cycle begins to break.

5. Projection and the Recurrence of the "Other"

In the intricate dance of human relationships, we often find ourselves reacting intensely to certain individuals, attributing to them qualities or intentions that may not align with their reality.

This phenomenon, known as projection, serves as a mirror reflecting our own unconscious thoughts, feelings, or desires onto others. It's a defence mechanism that allows us to externalize internal conflicts, making them more manageable by perceiving them as originating from the outside world.

Sigmund Freud introduced the concept of projection as a means by which individuals defend themselves against their own unacceptable impulses by attributing them to others. He posited that this mechanism helps alleviate the anxiety associated with internal conflicts by displacing them outward. For instance, a person harbouring aggressive tendencies might perceive others as hostile, thereby justifying their own aggression as a defensive response.

Carl Jung expanded upon Freud's ideas, suggesting that projection is not merely a defence mechanism but also a fundamental process through which we engage with the unconscious. He believed that by recognizing and withdrawing our projections, we could achieve greater self-awareness and personal growth.

Jung stated:
"Everything that is unconscious in ourselves we discover in our neighbour, and we treat him accordingly".

Contemporary research supports these notions, indicating that projection is a common psychological process. Studies have shown that individuals often project their own undesirable traits onto others, especially when attempting to suppress these traits within themselves. This projection can lead to distorted perceptions and strained interpersonal relationships.

Moreover, projection plays a significant role in the formation of the "Other", a concept wherein individuals or groups are perceived as fundamentally different and often inferior. This process can lead to prejudice, discrimination, and conflict, as the projected negative qualities are seen as inherent to the "Other" rather than as reflections of one's own unconscious content.

Understanding projection and its impact on our perceptions of others is crucial for personal development and fostering healthier relationships. By acknowledging our projections, we can begin to dismantle the barriers they create, allowing for more authentic connections and a deeper understanding of ourselves.

6. The Myth of Moving On

In modern culture, healing is often portrayed as a straight line: a goal to reach, a phase to finish, a badge of honor that proves we've transcended pain. The phrase "move on" echoes everywhere, from well-meaning friends to motivational quotes. But the psyche is not a spreadsheet, and the soul does not run on timelines.

Both Freud and Jung understood that repression, the act of banishing uncomfortable emotions from conscious awareness, does not equate to resolution. Freud described repression as the cornerstone of neurosis. What is pushed down reemerges elsewhere: in dreams, slips of the tongue, irrational fears, or recurring patterns. "The mind is like an iceberg," he said. "It floats with one-seventh of its bulk above water."

Jung agreed that what remains unconscious does not simply vanish. But while Freud believed that bringing repressed material into awareness was largely enough for healing, Jung argued that *integration* is the deeper task. Awareness alone is not transformation. The shadow must be befriended, its messages deciphered, and its power harnessed, not merely exposed.

This is where the myth of moving on becomes dangerous. It creates the illusion that time alone is a healer. That to forget is to heal. That silence is strength. In truth, unresolved wounds fester beneath the surface, shaping our relationships, decisions, and self-worth in subtle but profound ways. They manifest not as dramatic breakdowns, but as low-level dissatisfaction, recurring conflicts, or an inability to feel joy.

Modern psychology echoes this. Studies in trauma therapy, from pioneers like Bessel van der Kolk and Gabor Maté, reveal that the body holds memory in ways the mind cannot access through logic alone. "The body keeps the score," van der Kolk writes, referencing how trauma continues to express itself in physical symptoms, emotional reactivity, and even immune response.

To "move on" implies a forward motion without turning back. But shadow work insists that we *turn inward*. That we go back, not to get stuck, but to retrieve what we abandoned. The crying child. The unspoken grief. The denied truth. We revisit not to regress, but to reclaim. We return so that we can, at last, go forward whole.

The myth of moving on also reinforces the performance of healing. We tell ourselves and others that we're "fine," even when the echo of an old story still lives in our chest. This façade keeps us isolated. We compare our mess to someone else's mask and conclude that we are broken. But real healing is rarely tidy. It is cyclical, sacred, and often silent.

In Jungian terms, to heal is not to escape the shadow but to bring it into the light of the Self. And sometimes, what we think of as regression is actually deep integration. Not every tear is a setback. Not every trigger is a failure. Some are doorways.

Healing is not about moving on. It's about moving *in*, into the place where pain still waits to be witnessed. Into the story we keep trying to bury. And when we finally meet it with compassion, something shifts.

We don't move on. We move through. And in doing so, we carry forward something far more powerful than closure. We carry integration.

7. The Unconscious as Destiny

There is a quiet force that guides so many of our choices, relationships, and reactions, not fate, not randomness, but the unconscious. Long before we choose consciously, we are pulled by patterns we cannot see, echoing unresolved histories and inherited wounds. Jung's enduring statement, "Until you make the unconscious conscious, it will direct your life, and you will call it fate," captures this reality with chilling clarity.

To Jung, the unconscious was not merely a storage bin of forgotten material but a dynamic, purposeful system within the psyche, rich with instinct, memory, symbol, and potential. It was both a map of our past and a mirror of our wholeness. In contrast, Freud saw the unconscious primarily as a repository of repressed drives, particularly sexual and aggressive urges. For him, the unconscious was the engine of neurosis, a domain that needed to be made known and domesticated through analysis.

But where Freud leaned toward determinism, Jung saw a kind of teleology, a forward movement in the psyche seeking integration. He believed that the unconscious was not only shaped by what we repress but also by what we long to become. Dreams, for Jung, were not just wish fulfillments or disguised desires. They were messages from the Self, encoded in archetypal imagery, offering clues to wholeness. They whispered truths that the ego was not yet ready to speak aloud.

When we are unaware of these inner messages, when we deny our grief, rage, shame, or longing, they do not disappear. Instead, they guide us silently. The unresolved trauma may choose our partner. The unacknowledged fear may choose our job. The denied shadow may choose our politics, our addictions, our patterns of escape. We call it bad luck or fate. But often, it is simply the unconscious asserting itself.

This is why shadow work is not a spiritual luxury; it is psychological necessity. Without it, we live on repeat. We become actors in scripts we didn't write, reenacting themes of abandonment, betrayal, or powerlessness. Not because we want to, but because we haven't yet reclaimed the authorship of our lives.

In Jungian terms, fate becomes choice only when we meet the unconscious halfway. Only then can the symbols shift. Only then can the dream change. The unconscious, once feared or pathologized, becomes a guide.

Freud, ever the empiricist, warned against the mystification of the psyche. He remained sceptical of any idea that suggested the unconscious was creative or sacred. Yet Jung saw it as exactly that, a sacred terrain within, where the soul speaks in image and emotion, asking to be remembered.

> *"The privilege of a lifetime is to become who you truly are."*
> ~ *Carl Gustav Jung*

To ignore the unconscious is to hand over the reins of life to forces we do not understand. But to face it, to listen to it, work with it, integrate it, is to step into the profound responsibility of freedom.

Not freedom from pain or complexity, but freedom from repetition. From projection. From the false life.

When we do not make the unconscious conscious, we live reactively. When we do, we live symbolically. And in that shift, destiny is rewritten, not in dramatic gestures, but in subtle daily choices that align us with the truth of who we are.

8. Returning to the Scene, Reclaiming the Self

There is a moment in deep inner work when we circle back, not to punish ourselves, not to relive the pain, but to retrieve the part of us that never left. The psyche, unlike the ego, does not move in straight lines. It moves in spirals. Healing, then, is not about finally escaping the past, it's about turning toward the moment we split from ourselves and daring to step back in with new eyes.

Freud once remarked, "No mortal can keep a secret. If his lips are silent, he chatters with his fingertips; betrayal oozes out of him at every pore." Though his analysis emphasized repressed memory and its symptomatic return, he did not believe that healing required returning to the actual event. He focused instead on the analytic process of interpretation, bringing the repressed content into language and narrative so it could lose its hold.

Jung agreed that the forgotten must be remembered. But he also believed that the "scene" of psychological injury is not a single event, it is a symbolic rupture. It is the place where the Self was exiled, often long before we had words. To return to this place is not simply to recall facts, but to reconnect with the essence we abandoned to survive. It is the place of fragmentation, yes, but also the place of retrieval.

This is the sacred paradox: we must go back to go forward. The wound holds the key. Not because pain is noble, but because truth lives there. And when we dare to meet the moment when we first felt unwanted, unheard, unseen, something ancient within us exhales.

In trauma-informed therapy, this return is often called "reprocessing." In Jungian analysis, it may emerge through active imagination, dreamwork, or symbolic ritual. In both, the goal is not catharsis, it is reintegration. We do not revisit the past to get stuck in it. We revisit to welcome back the part of us still waiting there, still believing the story ended in rejection, abandonment, shame.

To reclaim the Self is to reparent the psyche, to offer what was missing not just externally, but internally. Affirmation. Compassion. Curiosity. And most of all, presence. We cannot change what happened. But we can change what we believe about ourselves because of what happened. And that change rewrites the nervous system. It softens the fear. It reshapes the future.

Jung called this process "individuation", becoming who we truly are by integrating all that we are. The exile becomes the guide. The forgotten becomes the foundation. What once broke us open becomes the gateway.

> *"The most terrifying thing is to accept oneself completely."*
> ~ *Carl Gustav Jung*

This kind of healing is not loud. It does not need applause. It is the quiet courage to stand in the ruins and plant something new. It is to walk back to the place we froze, not to re-live the terror, but to unfreeze the soul. To touch the scar not with judgment, but with reverence. And to say, "I'm here now. We made it through."

9. Echoes No More

There comes a time in the work of inner healing when the echo fades, not because the past is forgotten, but because it is no longer dictating the present. The sound of an old belief, a buried shame, a repeating pattern once rang through every corridor of the psyche. But now it softens. Not silenced by suppression but quieted by integration. When the psyche is heard, it does not need to shout.

Freud believed the past was the blueprint. That by analysing one's childhood, especially through the lens of desire, repression, and the Oedipal complex, we could uncover the root of neurosis and treat it through insight. In his view, the echo of the past was inevitable, and analysis was the scalpel to cut the pattern.

Jung, however, came to believe that the past, while important, was not the only architect of the psyche. He saw the unconscious not just as a storehouse of memory and repression, but as a creative force, a reservoir of symbols, dreams, and sacred images pulling us toward integration. He wrote, *"Your vision will become clear only when you can look into your own heart. Who looks outside dreams, who looks inside awakens."*

And this is where the divide becomes unmistakable.

Freud taught us to excavate the ruins. Jung invited us to rebuild from them. Freud mapped the libido; Jung sought the soul. Freud explained pathology; Jung offered transformation. To Freud, the psyche was a conflict of impulses. To Jung, it was a call to wholeness.

This is not to diminish Freud's brilliance. Without his fearless inquiry into the unconscious, the door might never have opened.

But Jung walked through it, and what he found was not just repression, but redemption.

As the author, I must pause here and ask you, who are you letting narrate your inner world?

Is it the voice that says your life is shaped by buried urges and outdated scripts? Or the one that whispers there is more to you, more story, more soul, more Self yet to be remembered?

This chapter has not asked you to take sides. It has asked you to listen. To feel, to reflect, and to notice when the same wound keeps speaking. The echo is not proof you are broken. It is proof something inside you is still waiting to be welcomed home.

The difference between Freud and Jung at this point is not academic, it is existential. One invites you to deconstruct your past. The other invites you to reconstruct your wholeness.

Let the echo fade. Let the Self return. You are not the sum of your symptoms. You are the witness of your shadow, and the artist of your becoming.

> *"One does not become enlightened by imagining figures of light, but by making the darkness conscious."*
> *~ Carl Gustav Jung*

From Shadow to Symbol

The Future of Inner Work

The Rise of the Inner Renaissance

The tides have turned. What was once dismissed as mystical, or marginal is now part of a larger renaissance. In an age of overstimulation and digital facades, the language of depth, the language of the soul, is returning. And with it, shadow work has evolved beyond the confines of clinical psychology or spiritual subcultures. It is becoming a symbol of something more: the collective hunger to be whole.

Just decades ago, the idea of inner darkness was something to suppress or sanitize. Freud, with his emphasis on biological instinct and repression, laid a foundational lens: the psyche as a machine of drives and defences, to be analysed and interpreted. Jung, in contrast, saw something more fluid, more expansive, a symbolic system always reaching toward balance. This philosophical divide now reemerges in our time, not as a battle between ideas, but as a choice for those seeking depth.

In 2025, shadow work is no longer hidden. It pulses through therapy rooms, social media reels, podcasts, and quiet journal entries. This movement signals more than personal transformation, it reflects a cultural yearning for authenticity and presence. Where once we chased optimization and constant productivity, many now turn inward for something truer. This is future pacing with a soul. We are not escaping, we are returning.

It is not accidental. It is archetypal. The psyche, overwhelmed by data and disembodied interaction, begins to call itself back. And in that calling, Jung's mythopoetic lens becomes not just relevant, it becomes vital. We're not just integrating trauma. We're reclaiming story. We're not fixing a broken mind. We're meeting a fractured myth.

From Wound to Wisdom

This language shift, from pathology to possibility, is no small thing. It marks a turning point in how we view the shadow itself. Freud viewed neurosis as the return of the repressed, requiring dissection and dialogue. Jung took the same terrain and asked, What if the wound is not just pain, but also potential? This reframe is empowering, and it's why so many now view shadow work as sacred, not clinical.

The stories we carry are not just wounds, they are wisdom encoded in memory, image, and behaviour. To meet the shadow is not to exile it but to learn its dialect. The anxious thought might contain the lost child. The addictive craving might mask the ungrieved death. The outburst might hold the voice we weren't allowed to use. Freud traced these symptoms to history. Jung invited us to sit beside them and listen.

Symbolism Over Symptom

We live in a world obsessed with labels. Symptom clusters, diagnostic codes, algorithmic suggestions. But beneath it all, the psyche is not speaking in spreadsheets, it is speaking in symbols. Dreams, myths, synchronicities, and images continue to surface in the inner lives of those doing shadow work. This is the curiosity gap we must enter: why do so many modern people, during scientific materialism, still dream of snakes, oceans, and forgotten homes?

Jung would say: because the soul never stopped speaking. Freud might suggest: the return of the repressed, dressed in metaphor. Yet where Freud stopped at symbolism as disguise, Jung saw the symbol as revelation. In today's resurgence of dream journaling, tarot, somatic art, and archetypal therapy, we witness the reemergence of the symbolic mind. Not as escape, but as return.

Wholeness as Revolution

In a fragmented world, wholeness is a revolutionary act. This pattern recognition is the core of modern shadow work: noticing how everything we cast out eventually loops back. Cancel culture. Burnout. Disconnection. These aren't isolated events. They are symptoms of collective shadow projection.

Freud might interpret these through the lens of sublimated aggression or displaced libido. Jung would ask what soul was missing in the system.

This distinction is no longer theoretical, it's personal. When we own our anger, we stop projecting enemies. When we face our grief, we stop fearing endings. When we befriend our inner exiles, we stop recreating abandonment. Shadow work is no longer just about healing wounds. It's about reclaiming the capacity for nuance and compassion. It is wholeness not as performance, but as path.

The Soul Reclaims Its Seat

We are tired of the performative healing era. We are tired of the algorithmic fixes. Freud warned that religion was an illusion, a collective neurosis. Jung believed that the spiritual impulse was innate, a fundamental movement of the psyche. Today, people are not returning to organized religion in droves. But they are returning to soul. They are learning to sit with mystery, to slow down, to honor their dreams, their ancestors, their intuition.

This is not regression.

It is reintegration. And it is relatable because most of us are burnt out from optimization. We want what's real. We want the part of us that doesn't need a filter. Jung's symbolic Self offers that anchor: a centre not shaped by approval, but by inner truth. A compass that no algorithm can predict.

The Return of Ritual

Rituals are returning in unexpected ways. Through quiet journaling practices. Through full-moon circles. Through online grief communities. Through the sacred stillness of putting away your phone and breathing into your body. Freud saw ritual as compulsive, neurotic. Jung saw it as a container for transformation.

This longing for ritual is a longing for structure in the midst of chaos. A longing for rhythm in a world of endless scroll. Shadow work, at its best, now includes rituals of re-entry. Daily reflections. Symbolic actions. Embodied movement. All of them remind us: the soul is not abstract. It needs form. It needs attention. It needs time.

Inner Work as Collective Antidote

Shadow work is not just for self-help. It is for world healing. When you stop projecting your pain, you stop creating enemies. When you name your fear, you stop needing to dominate. This reciprocity, the shift from blame to responsibility, is the soul of collective evolution.

Freud may have focused on intrapsychic drives, but Jung saw the psyche in relationship to everything: history, culture, ancestry, future. This systemic awareness is now seeping into leadership models, parenting philosophies, trauma-informed activism. Inner work is the antidote, not because it saves the world, but because it stops us from repeating it.

Shadow, Reimagined

It's time to stop pathologizing the parts of us that don't fit. To stop naming our truth a disorder. This identity expansion is the new wave of shadow work, one that embraces contradiction, complexity, and fluidity. We are not broken. We are layered. Freud categorized. Jung witnessed.

And now, we reclaim the language.

We rewrite the myth. We see the anxious one not as broken, but as alert. We see the angry one not as dangerous, but as drawing a boundary. We see the withdrawn one not as apathetic, but as discerning. The new language of self is emerging, and it is tender, symbolic, and whole.

The Soul Ahead: Jung's Vision Reborn

Freud gave us the courage to look at the mind. Jung gave us the courage to look at the soul.

Today, shadow work invites us to look at both, and to imagine something more. Not a cure, but a conversation. Not an endpoint, but an evolution.

The future of shadow work will not belong to any one theory. It will belong to those who listen. Who integrate. Who dare to walk inward not to escape, but to return. Let this be your invitation:

To make the darkness conscious. To greet the unseen. To meet the Self. Not as an idea, but as a lived, sacred rhythm.

> *"The privilege of a lifetime is to become who you truly are."*
> ~ Carl Gustav Jung

> *"We are what we are because we have been what we have been."*
> ~ Sigmund Freud

Two truths.

One journey.

The choice is yours.

Post Reading Reflection

Choosing the Path Within

The Shadow at the Crossroads ~ Choosing Your Compass

You've reached the end of this journey, but in truth, it's only the beginning. Not of someone else's legacy, not of Freud's or Jung's theories, but of your own path inward. Shadow work, as you've now seen, is not a destination. It's a mirror held to your inner world, asking only one thing, will you look honestly?

Throughout this book, you've walked between two worlds. Freud led you into the mechanics of repression, drive, and instinct, he named what society couldn't say. Jung invited you further in, where symbols whispered through dreams and archetypes rose from the depths. Now you stand at a crossroads. One path leads toward decoding the symptom. The other, toward reclaiming your soul.

This is your compass moment. The theories were never the point. The question is, what do they awaken in you?

Legacy of the Mind ~ Legacy of the Soul

As you reflect, you can see it clearly now. Freud offered the language of the hidden: neurosis, defence, the unconscious machinery of desire. He held up a mirror to modern life, exposing what we repress and why. But often, what he showed reflected back dysfunction.

Jung, on the other hand, turned the mirror into a window. He saw the unconscious not as a chamber of conflict but a deep well of wisdom. Where Freud saw symptoms to analyse, Jung saw symbols to explore. Freud described. Jung mythologized. One gave us the mind. The other, the soul.

Both men left you tools. But only you can decide which ones resonate. Or perhaps your truth lies between them.

Integration Begins in Daily Life

You don't need a couch or a clinician to begin. Shadow work is here, in the rawness of your daily life. It's in the argument that leaves you silent in the car. It's in the ache that rises when you scroll past a curated joy that doesn't feel like yours. It's in the way you speak, or don't, during hard moments in your relationships.

Freud would have you trace these patterns to childhood memories, seeking the original wound. Jung would nudge you to ask what part of your Self was exiled in that moment. Either way, shadow work is not an intellectual exercise. It is a felt experience. It is the pause between reaction and reflection. It is the courage to stay in the discomfort, long enough to hear what it's really trying to teach you.

The Return of the Inner Healer ~ From Theory to Soul Practice

You may have noticed it: the longing for depth. The desire to slow down. The impulse to honor what you feel, not just fix it. That's the voice of your inner healer, and it's more than a metaphor. It's the psychic reality that Freud's analysis pointed toward and Jung's soul work brought to life.

You don't need to choose between science and spirit. The modern psyche holds both. Therapy, ritual, journaling, somatic breathwork, ancestral reconnection, all of these are invitations. You build an altar in the pages of your notebook. You find stillness in three conscious breaths before dinner. You learn to hold your humanity, not dissect it.

The Sacred Responsibility of Wholeness

Wholeness is not about perfection. It's about responsibility. You didn't choose all your wounds, but you get to choose how they end. Freud gave us insight into how trauma travels across generations. Jung expanded the view, showing us how we all swim in a collective unconscious filled with inherited patterns.

Now the responsibility is yours. To become the one who breaks the pattern. The one who stops blaming and starts healing. The one who pauses before passing on the pain. You don't have to fix the world. But you can stop it from repeating through you.

Final Words: The Inner Journey Is the Human Journey

Here you are. On the final page. And still, at the very beginning. This is the real nature of shadow work. It's not about transcending who you are. It's about remembering. You were never meant to become someone else. You were always meant to return to the truth you already carry.

Freud and Jung gave us maps. They disagreed, they diverged, and yet, each offered a way inward. You may lean toward Freud's logic or Jung's symbolism. Or you may take what serves from both. That's not a betrayal. That's integration.

So pause here. Not to close the book, but to open the door. To choose the path that calls you forward, not into perfection, but into presence.

"The privilege of a lifetime is to become who you truly are."
~ *Carl Gustav Jung*

That's your invitation now. With you on this path,
~ *Jason A. Solomon*, B.Ed.

The Mirror of Harry

Harry never spoke of his adoption. Not openly. It was one of those facts buried under layers of polite dinner talk and family traditions that never felt like his own. He was brought into a family that made sure his physical needs were met, clothes, education, a roof, but love was rationed. Affection went to the "real children," the bloodline. He was the outsider tucked into family portraits, the addendum to their legacy.

Freud would have studied Harry and pointed to repressed sexuality. Perhaps the lack of a mother's warmth had interfered with his Oedipal development, creating what Freud called a 'failure of normal sexual maturation.' In Freud's eyes, Harry's emotional aloofness and superficial relationships could be traced back to an unresolved castration complex. His avoidance of intimacy? A defence mechanism, masking latent anxiety stemming from unconscious sexual conflict. Harry's internal struggle would be diagnosed, interpreted, reduced to sexual frustration and unresolved childhood desire.

But something about that felt... incomplete.

Harry had indeed grown into a man wary of closeness. Two marriages dissolved under the pressure of his emotional silence. His partners wanted vulnerability; he offered solutions. They cried; he shut down. One of them called him a "ghost with a heartbeat." He remembered that line more than anything else.

Jung would have met Harry differently.

Instead of dissecting Harry's libido, Jung would have sat beside the wound. He might have asked, "What dream keeps returning? What symbol haunts you?" Harry's answer would have surprised him. For months, he'd been dreaming of an old house, one he didn't recognize but felt drawn to. Each time, a locked room waited upstairs. He never entered it. He always woke up.

Jung would call this house a symbol of the Self. The locked room? The place where Harry's disowned parts had waited, silent and forgotten. Not just sexual repression, but the ache of never belonging. The pain of feeling like a guest in his own childhood. The deep, soul-level grief of being denied the birthright of unconditional love.

This wasn't about the phallus. It was about the fracture.

As Harry began to explore his dreams and memories with someone who didn't try to fix him, something softened. He recalled how, as a child, he once tried to run away. He packed two sandwiches and a matchbox car. He was six. He only made it to the edge of the garden. No one noticed. He cried into his knees until the sun went down, then returned to a house where no one asked where he'd been.

Freud might call this an attention-seeking behaviour. Jung would call it the soul's first attempt to be seen.

Over time, Harry stopped trying to 'solve' his sadness. He began to witness it. To walk with it. He journaled without editing. He listened to music that made him cry. He stopped performing strength and started practicing presence. And one night, in a dream, he finally opened the door.

Inside the room was not horror, not shame, but a younger version of himself, sitting quietly, waiting. Harry walked over. Sat beside him. Didn't say a word.

Shadow Work Evolution – Why Jung Followed the Freudian Fear!

This is the heart of shadow work. Freud taught us that our darkness must be interpreted. Jung reminded us it must also be felt.

Harry's story is not unique. It is the story of anyone who was emotionally orphaned, who learned to hide their truth to survive. It is the story of those who were told to be grateful, when they were simply longing to be loved.

In the shadow, Harry found not a diagnosis, but a doorway.

And this is where the theories diverge. Freud offered the key to pathology. Jung offered the map to the sacred.

Harry chose to walk deeper, not to fix what was broken, but to meet what had always been there.

And in doing so, he became not someone new, but someone whole.

Endnotes & References

1. Freud and Jung Primary Texts

- Freud, Sigmund. *The Interpretation of Dreams.* 1899. (1900). London: Hogarth Press.
- Freud, Sigmund. *Three Essays on the Theory of Sexuality.* 1905.
- Freud, Sigmund. *Civilization and Its Discontents.* 1930.
- Jung, Carl Gustav. *The Archetypes and the Collective Unconscious.* Collected Works Vol. 9 Part 1, Princeton University Press.
- Jung, Carl Gustav. *Psychological Types.* Collected Works Vol. 6, Princeton University Press.
- Jung, Carl Gustav. *The Undiscovered Self.* Princeton University Press, 1957.
- Jung, Carl Gustav. *Memories, Dreams, Reflections.* Recorded and edited by Aniela Jaffé. 1962.

2. The Freud–Jung Correspondence

- McGuire, William (Ed.). The Freud/Jung Letters: The Correspondence between Sigmund Freud and C.G. Jung. Princeton University Press, 1974.

3. Key Theoretical and Academic References

- Ellenberger, Henri F. The Discovery of the Unconscious: The History and Evolution of Dynamic Psychiatry. Basic Books, 1970.
- Shamdasani, Sonu. Jung and the Making of Modern Psychology: The Dream of a Science. Cambridge University Press, 2003.
- Hillman, James. Re-Visioning Psychology. Harper Perennial, 1975.
- Neumann, Erich. The Origins and History of Consciousness. Princeton University Press, 1954.
- Bishop, Paul. Analytical Psychology and German Classical Aesthetics: Goethe, Schiller, and Jung. Routledge, 2007.

4. Cultural and Symbolic Analysis

- Campbell, Joseph. *The Hero with a Thousand Faces*. Princeton University Press, 1949.
- Estés, Clarissa Pinkola. *Women Who Run With the Wolves*. Ballantine Books, 1992.
- Kalsched, Donald. *The Inner World of Trauma: Archetypal Defences of the Personal Spirit*. Routledge, 1996.

5. Trauma, Neuroscience & Modern Shadow Work

- van der Kolk, Bessel. The Body Keeps the Score: Brain, Mind, and Body in the Healing of Trauma. Penguin, 2014.
- Siegel, Daniel J. The Developing Mind: How Relationships and the Brain Interact to Shape Who We Are. Guilford Press, 2012.
- Mate, Gabor. In the Realm of Hungry Ghosts: Close Encounters with Addiction. Vintage Canada, 2008.

- Levine, Peter A. Waking the Tiger: Healing Trauma. North Atlantic Books, 1997.

6. Additional Digital & Multimedia References

- Amanda Todd, "My Story: Struggling, Bullying, Suicide, Self Harm." YouTube, 2012. https://www.youtube.com/watch?v=vOHXGNx-E7E
- 7. Specific Quotation and Symbolic Interpretation Notes
- (§274) indicates section numbers from Carl Jung's *Collected Works*, not page numbers.
- Freud's quotes and terminology around repression, neurosis, and libido appear primarily in *Three Essays on the Theory of Sexuality* and *Civilization and Its Discontents*.
- Jung's descriptions of individuation, the Self, and archetypal psychology are drawn from *The Archetypes and the Collective Unconscious* and *The Undiscovered Self*.

8. Selected Quotations Cited in Chapter Openings and Final Reflections

- Jung: "The privilege of a lifetime is to become who you truly are." (*Collected Works*, CW Vol. 7).
- Freud: "We are what we are because we have been what we have been." (*New Introductory Lectures on Psychoanalysis*, 1933).
- Jung: "Who looks outside, dreams, who looks inside, awakens." (*The Undiscovered Self*, 1957).

Glossary of Terms

Analytic Psychology
Founded by Carl Jung, this branch of psychology emphasizes the exploration of the unconscious, the role of symbolic imagery, dreams, and the process of individuation.

Anima / Animus
Terms coined by Jung referring to the unconscious feminine qualities in men (anima) and unconscious masculine qualities in women (animus), representing internal gender polarity and psychological balance.

Archetypes
Universal patterns or symbolic figures (e.g., the Hero, the Mother, the Shadow) residing in the collective unconscious. Archetypes shape human experience and are revealed in dreams, myths, and behaviour.

Catharsis
Emotional release that occurs when repressed memories or unconscious feelings are brought to consciousness and expressed.

Collective Unconscious
A foundational Jungian concept describing the inherited layer of the unconscious mind shared among all humans, containing archetypes and universal symbolic imagery.

Compensation
In Jungian theory, the unconscious often compensates for

imbalances in the conscious mind, such as inflating dreams in someone with low self-esteem.

Complex
A cluster of emotionally charged ideas or memories, often formed around a central theme (e.g., the mother complex), that can influence behaviour unconsciously.

Defence Mechanisms
Freudian concept referring to unconscious psychological strategies (e.g., denial, projection, repression) that protect the ego from anxiety or unacceptable thoughts.

Dreamwork
The process of interpreting dreams to access unconscious material. For Jung, dreams are messages from the unconscious, rich with symbolic guidance.

Ego
In Freudian terms, the rational, decision-making part of the mind. In Jungian terms, the centre of consciousness that navigates between the inner and outer world.

Id
According to Freud, the primitive part of the psyche driven by instinctual desires, operating on the pleasure principle.

Individuation
A core Jungian process of integrating the conscious and unconscious aspects of the psyche to achieve psychological wholeness.

Inner Child
A concept representing the vulnerable, emotional part of ourselves shaped by early childhood experiences, often a focus in shadow work and healing.

Libido
Freud's term for the instinctual psychic energy derived primarily from sexual drives. Jung later expanded it to include life energy and creative drive.

Neurosis
A condition characterized by emotional distress and inner conflict, often stemming from repressed unconscious material.

Persona
Jung's term for the social mask or identity one presents to the world. It often conceals the deeper, truer Self.

Projection
A defence mechanism in which one attributes unwanted feelings or traits onto others. For Jung, projection can be a path to self-awareness.

Psyche
The totality of the human mind, conscious and unconscious. Jung viewed the psyche as an evolving system striving toward balance and meaning.

Repression
Freud's concept referring to the unconscious exclusion of painful or unacceptable thoughts from conscious awareness.

Shadow
The repressed, denied, or hidden aspects of oneself. For Jung, the shadow is both personal and collective, and integration of the shadow is essential for growth.

Shadow Work
The practice of exploring, understanding, and integrating the disowned parts of the self. It involves honesty, self-inquiry, and emotional courage.

Superego
Freud's concept for the internalized moral standards and societal rules, which govern behaviour and generate guilt when violated.

Synchronicity
Jung's term for meaningful coincidences that are not causally connected but carry personal or archetypal significance.

Transference
A psychoanalytic concept where a person projects feelings about important figures from their past onto a therapist or other individuals.

Trauma-Informed
An approach that acknowledges the lasting effects of trauma on a person's body, mind, and behaviour, and integrates safety, empathy, and non-retraumatization into therapeutic work.

Unconscious
The part of the mind not accessible to conscious awareness. Freud focused on repressed material; Jung expanded it to include creative, symbolic content.

Expanded Explanation of Key Terms

1. Archetypes

In Jungian psychology, archetypes are universal, inherited symbols or patterns that exist in the collective unconscious of all humans. These symbols manifest across cultures through myths, dreams, literature, art, and personal behaviour. They are not learned but are *inborn psychological blueprints* that influence how we experience the world.

For example:

- The **Mother** archetype represents nurturing, protection, and unconditional love.

- The **Hero** archetype symbolizes courage, sacrifice, and personal transformation.

- The **Shadow** archetype holds repressed traits and the darker, less conscious aspects of the self.

Jung believed archetypes are living components of the psyche, shaping our perceptions and choices even when we are unaware of them.

Synonyms and Alternative Phrases:

- Symbolic Patterns
- Mythic Templates
- Inner Storylines
- Psychological Blueprints
- Primordial Images
- Universal Characters
- Collective Motifs
- Narrative Frameworks of the Psyche
- Unconscious Scripts

2. Jungian

The term *Jungian* refers to the ideas and psychological framework developed by Carl Gustav Jung, a Swiss psychiatrist and psychoanalyst who founded Analytical Psychology. His work diverged from Sigmund Freud's by incorporating spirituality, myth, and symbolism as essential to understanding the human psyche.

Jungian thought emphasizes:

- The *collective unconscious* (a shared psychic inheritance)
- The *individuation process* (becoming a whole, authentic self)
- The role of *dreams, symbols,* and *archetypes*
- The integration of opposites (e.g., conscious and unconscious, light and shadow)

It is a holistic and symbolic approach to psychology that values mystery, inner depth, and the soul's journey toward meaning.

Synonyms and Alternative Phrases:

- Depth-Oriented
- Symbolic Psychology
- Analytical Psychology (formal term)
- Inner Work Tradition
- Soul-Centred Psychology
- Archetypal Perspective
- Mythopoetic Psychology

3. Shadow Work

Shadow work is the intentional practice of exploring, confronting, and integrating the unconscious parts of oneself, especially those traits we hide, deny, or suppress. These may include fear, anger, shame, jealousy, or even positive qualities like power or creativity that we have rejected due to early conditioning or trauma.

Carl Jung described the *Shadow* as the "dark side" of the psyche, but not inherently evil. It is simply the part of us that is unseen. Shadow work involves meeting those parts with compassion, curiosity, and courage, transforming them into conscious allies rather than unconscious saboteurs.

Shadow work is not about perfection, it's about wholeness.

Synonyms and Alternative Phrases:

- Inner Integration

- Unconscious Exploration

- Emotional Unpacking

- Healing the Hidden Self

- Working with the Shadow

- Soul Excavation

- Reclaiming the Repressed

- Deep Self-Awareness Practices

- Shadow Integration

Symbol Index

A Jungian Lens on Inner Imagery

(A companion to the language of the psyche)

Carl Jung taught that symbols arise not from our intellect, but from the deeper currents of the unconscious. These images often appear in dreams, fantasies, or spontaneous thoughts, not as fixed meanings, but as living expressions of the psyche's inner truth.

The list below is not definitive. It is an invitation to explore, reflect, and attune to what each image means to *you*.

● Shadow

General Meaning: Repressed or denied aspects of the self
Jungian Insight: The shadow holds the traits we disown, fear, or judge. Encountering the shadow is essential for integration and wholeness.
Common Dreams/Symbols: Chases, confrontations, doppelgängers, masks

🐍 Snake

General Meaning: Transformation, fear, hidden knowledge
Jungian Insight: The serpent may represent both danger and sacred wisdom. It is often a symbol of potential rebirth when integrated consciously.

Common Dreams/Symbols: Shedding skin, coiling, sudden appearance

🌊 Ocean

<u>General Meaning</u>: Depth, emotion, the unknown
<u>Jungian Insight</u>: Often reflects the collective unconscious. Dreaming of water may symbolize being submerged in feeling, overwhelmed, or returning to source.
<u>Common Dreams/Symbols</u>: Drowning, floating, tidal waves

🔥 Fire

<u>General Meaning</u>: Destruction and purification
<u>Jungian Insight</u>: Fire may destroy illusions or ego structures, but also warm, awaken, and initiate. It often signals a psychic or spiritual breakthrough.
<u>Common Dreams/Symbols</u>: Houses burning, sacred flames, inner heat

👁 Mirror

<u>General Meaning</u>: Reflection of the self
<u>Jungian Insight</u>: The mirror may show what we cannot yet accept. Seeing oneself distorted or unfamiliar may indicate a shadow aspect coming into consciousness.
<u>Common Dreams/Symbols</u>: Broken mirrors, twin selves, silent faces

🦋 Butterfly

General Meaning: Change, impermanence, soul evolution
Jungian Insight: Often a messenger of transformation. It can appear during times of major life transition or after internal growth has taken place.
Common Dreams/Symbols: Emerging from cocoons, fluttering, following

🏠 House

General Meaning: The self or psyche
Jungian Insight: Rooms represent different aspects of the inner world. Basements often symbolize the unconscious; attics, memory; locked doors, repression.
Common Dreams/Symbols: Flooded rooms, missing stairs, moving house

☠ Death

General Meaning: Endings, transition, the unknown
Jungian Insight: Rarely literal, death in dreams often symbolizes the end of an identity, stage, or outdated belief. It precedes rebirth.
Common Dreams/Symbols: Funerals, graveyards, dying loved ones

🐺 Wolf

General Meaning: Wild instinct, danger, loyalty
Jungian Insight: The wolf may symbolize the primal self, both protective and predatory. In some dreams, it signals a call to reclaim instinctual wisdom.

Common Dreams/Symbols: Being hunted, running with a pack, lone wolf

🕯 Light

General Meaning: Illumination, clarity, truth
Jungian Insight: The presence of light suggests conscious awareness emerging. It can appear when something hidden is ready to be revealed or healed.
Common Dreams/Symbols: Candles, lanterns, sunrise

Comparative Symbol Index Table

Freud vs. Jung – Interpreting the Shadow through Symbolism

Symbol	Freud's Interpretation	Jung's Interpretation
Dreams	Manifestation of repressed desires (usually sexual or aggressive urges)	Expression of the unconscious using archetypes and meaningful symbolism
The Shadow	Repressed instinctual drives and forbidden desires	The unconscious parts of the personality needing integration
The Anima/Animus	Rarely emphasized or seen through gendered projection	Inner feminine (anima) or masculine (animus) archetype, guides toward wholeness
Mother Figure	Often central to Oedipal conflict; object of infantile desire	Archetype of nurturing and protection, or devouring control
Father Figure	Authority and fear; often source of guilt and suppression	Archetype of structure, wisdom, or oppression, depending on context
Sexual Symbols	Phallic or yonic symbols represent	Can carry multiple layers, sexual, spiritual, or transformative meanings

Symbol	Freud's Interpretation	Jung's Interpretation
	sexual frustration or desire	
Religion	A collective neurosis; illusion born from wish fulfillment	A symbolic structure pointing toward individuation and inner transformation
Myth & Folklore	Psychological disguise for primal urges	Universal symbolic expressions of the collective unconscious
Libido	Sexual energy that fuels behaviour and neuroses	General psychic energy that drives personal and spiritual growth
Therapeutic Goal	Catharsis and resolution of childhood conflict	Integration of unconscious material and alignment with the Self

Reflection Questions

A Personal Inquiry and Integration Guide

1. Which psychological lens resonated more deeply with you ~ Freud's emphasis on instinct and repression, or Jung's focus on integration and symbolism? Why?

2. When you reflect on your own life story, which parts do you suspect have been unconsciously suppressed or projected outward onto others?

3. How has your understanding of the 'shadow' changed while reading this book? What aspects of yourself might you now be willing to explore with more honesty?

4. In what ways did your upbringing, family dynamic, or cultural background shape your internalized ideas of what is 'acceptable' or 'unacceptable' in yourself?

5. Think of a recurring emotional pattern (e.g., anger, anxiety, avoidance). What symbolic meaning might this hold, beyond its surface-level expression?

6. If you could personify your shadow as a character, what would it look or sound like? What does it need from you to feel seen and integrated?

7. Have you ever experienced a dream, memory, or synchronicity that felt meaningful in ways you couldn't

explain? How might this relate to Jung's theory of archetypes and the symbolic Self?

8. How does your professional, educational, or personal role allow space for shadow work in others? Do you encourage, avoid, or suppress it? Why?

9. What inner 'other' have you been conditioned to exile or fear (your vulnerability, sexuality, rage, grief)? How might reclaiming that part change your relationships?

10. Freud explored how we are shaped by past drives; Jung explored how we are shaped by future potential. Which timeframe do you live in more often: past wounding, or future becoming?

11. Where in your life do you see the collective shadow manifesting today? How might individual healing contribute to cultural healing in that area?

12. If wholeness were your only goal, not perfection, not productivity, how would your choices, relationships, and daily rhythms shift?

13. What does 'integration' mean to you now, at the end of this book? How might you begin practicing it in small, consistent ways?

14. What parts of yourself do you still pathologize or label as 'wrong'? What happens when you view those same parts with curiosity instead of judgment?

15. How might your worldview change if you saw the psyche not as a problem to fix, but as a myth unfolding through your choices, dreams, and symbols?

Frequently Asked Questions

What exactly is "shadow work"?

Shadow work is the practice of becoming aware of and integrating the parts of yourself that you have repressed, denied, or hidden, often because they were deemed unacceptable by family, society, or culture. These may include emotions like anger, jealousy, grief, or shame, as well as desires, traits, or memories. The "shadow" is not inherently bad, it's simply unseen. The work involves bringing these parts into conscious awareness with compassion, not condemnation.

Is shadow work dangerous?

Shadow work is not inherently dangerous, but it *can* be destabilizing if rushed or done without support. The process can bring up old wounds, painful memories, or strong emotional reactions. For some, especially those with a history of trauma, it is important to engage in shadow work with a trained therapist or guide. The danger isn't in the shadow; it's in trying to confront it alone without the tools or support to hold what arises. Like any deep inner process, it requires care, patience, and boundaries.

Do therapists recommend shadow work?

Many therapists, especially those trained in Jungian, depth, or transpersonal psychology, support shadow work as a valuable part of healing. Others may use similar approaches under different names, such as "parts work," "inner child work," or "trauma integration." Not all therapeutic models explicitly reference Jung, but the idea of exploring the unconscious and integrating repressed material is widely respected. Always ask your therapist if shadow work aligns with their approach.

Is shadow work the same as trauma healing?

Not exactly, but they often overlap. Shadow work includes confronting aspects of self that may not be trauma-related, such as ego attachments, patterns of envy, resistance to vulnerability, or inherited beliefs. Trauma healing often focuses on restoring nervous system regulation and safety in the body. Both are complementary. Shadow work can help bring insight, while trauma work helps restore balance and resilience. Many practitioners now integrate both.

Can shadow work be spiritual?

Yes, and no. Shadow work can be deeply spiritual, especially in Jung's framework where the shadow is a portal to wholeness, authenticity, and connection with the symbolic Self. However, it can also be entirely secular, grounded in psychology and personal growth. The spiritual dimension is often a byproduct rather than a requirement. What matters is your intention: are you seeking insight, integration, awakening, or all three?

How do I know if I'm doing shadow work "right"?

If you are confronting uncomfortable truths with honesty and compassion rather than judgment or suppression, you're likely on the path. Shadow work is not about "fixing" yourself; it's about meeting what's hidden. Progress is not measured by perfection but by presence. You may notice changes in how you react, greater self-awareness, or the softening of old defences. That's a sign that integration is happening.

Do I have to relive my past to heal it?

Not always. Some memories or patterns may resurface, but reliving is not the goal. Jung emphasized symbolic understanding and the power of dreams, images, and archetypes to bring meaning to old pain. Shadow work is less about re-traumatizing and more about re-seeing. Sometimes insight alone is enough to shift a lifelong pattern. Other times, deeper healing requires body-based or therapeutic support.

Is it possible to go too far with shadow work?

Yes, especially if it becomes obsessive or self-punishing. Shadow work should deepen your humanity, not lead to self-loathing or isolation. Some people get stuck in a loop of endless self-analysis, mistaking intensity for insight. Others use shadow work as a form of emotional bypassing, an excuse to stay wounded or disconnected. Healthy shadow work includes *integration*, returning to daily life with more awareness, not staying in the dark.

What's the difference between shadow work and inner child work?

Inner child work often focuses on healing early emotional wounds, unmet needs, or developmental trauma. Shadow work can include this, but also addresses unconscious drives, projections, patterns, and aspects of identity that we disown as adults. The inner child might be one *expression* of the shadow, but the shadow also includes anger, sexuality, pride, envy, arrogance, and spiritual inflation. Shadow work is broader, but both approaches can work beautifully together.

When is the best time to begin shadow work?

There is no perfect time. But it often begins when something breaks through, an identity crisis, a relationship ending, burnout, grief, or simply the sense that you're no longer living authentically. The best time is when you feel safe enough to be honest, curious enough to explore, and supported enough to stay with what you find. Shadow work is not about fixing who you are. It's about remembering what you forgot.

How did Freud and Jung differ in their views on the unconscious?

Freud believed the unconscious was primarily a storage house of repressed thoughts, desires, and unresolved conflicts, mostly sexual or aggressive in nature. He saw it as a force to be uncovered, interpreted, and mastered. Jung agreed the unconscious held repressed material, but he also saw it as a *source of wisdom*, creativity, and symbolic meaning. He introduced the concept of the *collective unconscious*, suggesting that we carry universal psychic patterns (like myths and archetypes) shared across humanity.

Did Freud believe in the concept of the soul?

No. Freud was a scientific rationalist who believed that religion and spirituality were illusions, psychological crutches rooted in human fear and dependency. In his view, the mind was a system governed by instinctual drives and social constraints. Jung, however, believed the soul was central to the human experience. He saw spiritual development, dreams, and myth as essential tools in becoming whole. For Jung, the soul was not a doctrine, it was an unfolding mystery.

Why did Jung break away from Freud?

Jung's break from Freud stemmed from multiple philosophical differences. Freud emphasized sexual and aggressive drives as the core of human behaviour, whereas Jung believed the psyche was more complex, symbolic, and spiritually oriented. Jung rejected Freud's view that all psychic life could be reduced to libido and childhood trauma. Their split became inevitable when Jung began exploring topics like alchemy, religion, and archetypes, territories Freud dismissed as unscientific or mystical.

How would Freud and Jung interpret the same dream differently?

Freud would analyse a dream as the disguised fulfillment of a repressed wish, often related to sexuality, fear, or taboo. He would focus on the personal unconscious and interpret symbols through the lens of the dreamer's past. Jung, on the other hand, would consider the dream as a message from the unconscious that could guide the individual toward wholeness. He would look at both personal and *collective* symbols, believing that the dream's meaning could unfold over time rather than being strictly decoded.

Can I combine both Freud's and Jung's approaches in shadow work?

Absolutely. Many modern therapists and practitioners integrate both perspectives. Freud's model helps uncover formative patterns and defence mechanisms rooted in early life. Jung's model allows for symbolic, spiritual, and archetypal exploration. Together, they offer a more holistic view: one that acknowledges trauma and instinct while also honoring myth, meaning, and mystery. Shadow work today often blends these schools, bridging scientific insight with soulful integration.

Is shadow work safe for everyone to do?

Shadow work can be profoundly healing, but it's not always the right approach for every person at every time. For individuals experiencing acute trauma, crisis, or severe mental health symptoms, working with a qualified therapist is essential before diving into shadow exploration alone. The process can surface painful memories or emotional overwhelm. With the right support, however, it becomes a safe container for transformation.

What are the benefits of shadow work I should share with someone?

Shadow work can lead to greater emotional awareness, reduced reactivity, deeper self-compassion, and more authentic relationships. It allows people to break generational patterns, release internalized shame, and become more whole. By facing the parts of themselves they've rejected, individuals often experience relief, empowerment, and a renewed sense of purpose.

Are there risks in encouraging someone to do shadow work?

Yes, especially if it's done without preparation, support, or timing. Shadow work can unearth deep grief, suppressed anger, or trauma that someone may not be ready to face. Pushing a friend too quickly into shadow work can do more harm than good. The best approach is to offer resources, hold space, and emphasize that it's a personal choice. Timing and emotional readiness matter.

What if someone resists or denies their shadow?

Resistance is natural. The shadow often hides behind defence mechanisms like blame, distraction, or perfectionism. It takes courage to face what's uncomfortable or unflattering. If someone isn't ready or willing, respect their boundaries. The seed of insight often grows over time. Gentle reflection, not pressure, is usually the most helpful gift you can offer.

Can shadow work be done in community or should it stay private?

While shadow work begins as an inner journey, sharing insights in safe, supportive spaces can be transformative. Group therapy, conscious circles, or even one trusted friend can hold powerful mirrors. However, the process must be consensual and grounded. Vulnerability without safety can retraumatize. If you're advising someone, encourage them to discern carefully who they share their work with, and to always return to their own truth.

Afterword

When the Mirror Speaks Back

You've arrived here not by accident. If you've read this far, something in the pages spoke to you, whether softly or urgently, whether with the curiosity of the mind or the ache of the heart. Perhaps you've been holding questions. Perhaps you've been carrying pain. Either way, you came looking not just for answers, but for understanding. And that is the most human thing of all.

Shadow work has become a term that's bled into everyday conversations. Its hash tagged, aestheticized, shortened into TikTok-length tips. And yet, what you've discovered here, if you've truly read between the lines, is that shadow work is no trend. It is not a mood. It is not a self-help activity you tick off like exercise or diet. It is a descent. A reckoning. A resurrection.

I wrote this book not to give you easy steps, but to show you the ground you're standing on, and the layers beneath it. Because this work is real. It is ancient. And it can undo you if you're not ready or rebuild you if you are.

We began with two men. Sigmund Freud, who dared to look where no one else had looked, into the sexual, aggressive, compulsive drives that society represses. And Carl Gustav Jung, who dared to look even further, into the mystery behind those drives, into the dream, the myth, the soul.

Freud taught us to dissect the wound. Jung invited us to dialogue with it. And somewhere between their philosophies, between pathology and possibility, lies your truth.

Let me speak plainly now.

You will be told that shadow work is healing. And yes, it can be. But healing is not always soothing. Sometimes healing stings. Sometimes it burns. The shadow is not just your sadness or self-doubt. It is also your envy. Your rage. Your need to control. It is the image you've built to be loved, and the shame you buried to be accepted. The shadow is cunning; it wears the faces of your old beliefs. It mimics your defence mechanisms. It even hides inside your light.

Freud saw this with brutal honesty. He believed the unconscious was a battlefield of instincts, a cauldron of suppressed drives that leak out in dreams, slips of the tongue, and irrational behaviours. To him, every repression was a symptom, every symptom, a cipher. His goal was excavation. Dissection. Exposure. He taught us that until we make the unconscious conscious, it rules our lives without our consent.

But Freud stopped at repression. He viewed the psyche as a machine of instincts, primitive, mechanical, predictable. To Freud, healing meant control. It meant mastery over chaos.

Jung, however, investigated the same unconscious and saw not just a cesspool, but a cosmos. He believed that beyond neurosis lay meaning. That our symptoms were not just malfunctions, but messages. The shadow wasn't simply a threat; it was a gateway. Not to pathology, but to purpose.

You, dear reader, must now decide: Which lens do you wear? Do you view your pain as something to fix, or something to listen to? Do you want to decode your wounds, or transform them?

That choice has consequences.

Shadow work has consequences.

If you go in unprepared, you may stir what you cannot soothe. You may awaken memories without integration. You may find yourself flooded, not freed.

This is why I write this with caution. There is a danger in approaching the shadow with curiosity alone. You need courage. Structure. Timing. Safety. You need to know when to explore and when to pause. When to feel, and when to ground. Freud might call this resistance. Jung might call it rhythm. I call it discernment.

Let me give you a warning dressed in compassion:

Do not do this work in isolation. Shadow work is deeply personal, but it should never be purely private. Whether through a therapist, a wise elder, a somatic healer, or even a trusted friend, make sure you are witnessed. Make sure your echoes find a place to land.

The shadow feeds on secrecy. But it heals in relationship.

Now let's talk about where this shows up in your life.

You might think your anxiety is a problem to solve, but what if it's a compass pointing to the part of you that feels unsafe being seen? You might think your procrastination is laziness, but what if it's a signal that your identity has been hijacked by perfectionism and fear of failure?

Freud would ask: What childhood experience led to this block? What desire was repressed?

Jung would ask: What part of your Self has been banished? What story have you outgrown?

They're both right. And they're both incomplete. You are not just your trauma, and you are not just your potential. You are the tension between them.

If you've ever felt stuck in therapy, intellectualizing without transformation, it might be that you've been approaching your pain like a puzzle, not a presence. Freud's legacy leans heavily on interpretation. But interpretation without integration is like learning the story of fire without ever feeling its warmth.

Jung invites you to step into the fire.

To speak with your symbols. To paint your wounds. To ritualize your becoming.

This is why shadow work can't just be intellectual. It must be embodied. It must be emotional. And eventually, it must be spiritual. Not in the religious sense, but in the sense of remembering that your life has meaning beyond your survival.

This is where modern shadow work often goes wrong. It becomes a checklist. A series of journal prompts. A way to "level up" without ever melting down. But you cannot skip the dismemberment. You cannot bypass the body. Shadow work is not a life hack. It is a soul initiation.

And here's the paradox: when done right, it won't make you feel better, at least not right away. It may make you feel messier. More tender. More raw.

But that's the point. It peels you back to what is real.

So where do you begin?

You begin where you already are.

In the relationship that keeps triggering you.

In the shame you carry but don't understand.

In the dream that keeps repeating.

In the anger you judge.

In the grief you avoid.

In the inner voice that says, "There's more to me than this."

Begin there.

But don't end there.

Follow the thread. Track the emotion. Trace the memory. Let it speak.

Ask:

- What part of me is not allowed to exist?
- What am I most afraid they'll find out about me?
- When did I start hiding?

These are not casual questions. They will stir things up. So give yourself the dignity of depth. Don't rush it.

And know this: not everything in the shadow is dark. Some of your most radiant gifts were buried there. Your sensuality. Your creativity. Your intuition. Your joy. Shadow work is not just descent, it's retrieval.

This is where Jung's work shines.

He knew that the shadow, once faced, becomes the soil from which the Self emerges. That your most painful stories can become the myths you live with pride. That your sorrow can become a sacrament. That wholeness is not perfection, it is presence.

So, what now?

Now you walk.

Not with answers, but with awareness.

Not with force, but with faith.

You walk into your life more honest. More alert. More whole.

And if the path gets dark again, and it will, remember that you have a map. It is written in your dreams. It is felt in your body. It is etched in the ache that won't go away.

And you are not alone.

I stand with you, not as a guru, but as a fellow traveller. I wrote this book because I've lived the fragmentation. I've felt the numbness. I've wrestled with both Freud's ghost and Jung's invitation. And I chose to turn inward, not as escape, but as return.

If you've made it this far, I believe you are ready. Ready not for perfect healing, but for honest evolution. Ready not to become someone new, but to remember who you are beneath the masks.

You don't need to fix yourself. You need to face yourself.

Shadow work is not about becoming someone better.

It is about becoming someone real.

And that, more than any theory, changes everything.

With depth, solidarity, and quiet reverence,

~ Jason A. Solomon, B.Ed.
Author of *Shadow Work Evolution* and *365 Days of SOUL*

Shadow Work AI Companion

You can explore it here:

https://shadow-work.ai

Or

Scan the QR Code

The End

www.ingramcontent.com/pod-product-compliance
Lightning Source LLC
Chambersburg PA
CBHW070809100426
42742CB00012B/2306